An
8-track
church

in a CD world

The modern church in a postmodern world

To Bob Nash
missionary, father, friend
who always embraces the stranger

Robert N. Nash, Jr.
with foreword by Loren Mead

An
8-track
church
in a CD world

The modern church in a postmodern world

SMYTH&HELWYS
PUBLISHING, INCORPORATED · MACON, GEORGIA

Smyth & Helwys Publishing, Inc.
6316 Peake Road
Macon, Georgia 31210-3960
1-800-747-3016
©2001 by Smyth & Helwys Publishing

Library of Congress Cataloging-in-Publication Data

May, David M.
        An 8-track church in a cd world : the modern church in a postmodern
        world/ Robert N. Nash.
                p. cm.
        Includes bibliographical references.
        ISBN 1-57312-357-9 (pbk)
        1. Church renewal—United States
        2. Postmodernism—Religious aspects—Christianity
        I. Title

        BV600.2.N35 1997
        262'.001'7—dc21

                                                        97-11347
                                                        CIP

Contents

Foreword

Everyone who loves the church knows something's gone wrong. The neat packages and clear answers that made Christians so confident in earlier decades have become complex and confused. Those old enough to remember the church life of the 50s and 60s practice selective memory and have nostalgia for the way things "used to be." I say selective memory because that was a world in which many kinds of violence quietly disguised themselves as security and stability. Younger Christians have never had the experience of that illusory and triumphant age, so they wonder at the inability of their seniors to exorcise the spirit of those times and the customs of the church of those years.

Perhaps it is appropriate that this book bridges that generation gap—a son who loves the church dedicates his work to his father, who served the church in that older generation. And it is to the paradigmatic shift dramatized by the mind-blowing changes surfacing as these generations change that Robert Nash, Jr., addresses himself, opening doors for us to greet the possibilities of the future with hope, not dread.

Who in today's church has not sometimes wondered "why something just doesn't feel right about how we are 'doing church' these days." Some of us have even found ourselves saying to ourselves in self-doubt, "Am I crazy or what?" Some of what we seem to be doing in church feels like play-acting, but everybody else seems to take it all very seriously.

I am one who loves the church perhaps too much; and I am too eager to forgive its shortcomings because it means so much to me. It has nurtured and fed me in spite of its faults. Like Nash, I struggle[1] to make sense out of the changes that seem to sweep over our culture and threaten to make many things we do obsolete. Like Nash, I am convinced that what is going on is more than that some folks in the church have messed up. I am not of the opinion that we are likely to get very far trying to blame it all on some complex plot by people who have different positions on theology or politics or whatever. Many people in the churches are using up a lot of energy doing just that.

Nash is helpful to us in exploring the painful cultural divide we straddle—between a world he describes as the "modern world" and the world emerging around us, "the postmodern world."[2] He clarifies for us how it is that very change is shifting the ground under our feet, making obsolete the practices of yesterday, making obsolete even some of the institutional structures and the ways we have articulated the deepest things of our faith. It is not that those deep things of the faith have changed. Rather, the structures in which we housed them and the thought-forms with which we explained them have grown archaic. New language and new structures will be needed for gospel truth to be articulated in this world of postmodernity.

Our difficulty in responding to the need to change comes from our love of the familiar and our desire to protect valued practices and structures from the past. But even more, we resist the changes needed because we feel real threat in the ones we see coming down the pike. We are not as confident as we were a few decades ago when all the signs were optimistic.

Church leaders could once reassure us that we were on the right path because of the markers of success that surrounded what we did. Membership growth burgeoned everywhere. Our congregations built bigger and bigger sanctuaries and education buildings. Fate seemed to smile on us. The lack of those signs of success today has made us uncomfortable, unsure of ourselves. At one moment we want to try the old, familiar ways just a little harder to see if we can make it work once again. At the next moment we look for somebody to blame because it won't work.

One of the greatest strengths of this book is the new perspective it brings to the culture wars between traditionalists and progressivists. No battle has been more damaging to persons in the churches. It is a battle that has led to deep enmities and painful conflicts. Nash is sensitive in depicting the warring sides, but he helps us see that neither of them fully responds to the challenge before the churches now. The culture war between traditionalists and progressivists is a war using the tools and ideas of the modern world when we need ways of understanding one another in the postmodern world.

I appreciate the clues Nash gives about how to frame the new questions so we can get beyond whaling each other over the heads with the battle axes we used in ancient wars. He helps us see that both progressive and traditional Christians are called to go deeper and farther than their party positions have led them so far.

Nash also helps us see that the lack of success—in member growth and money and institutional aggrandizement—that makes us anxious is rooted not in our stupidity or error, but in deep changes in the culture around us and how it is shaped. He gives us clues about how to engage that culture in ways that are drawn from our roots in the biblical story and heritage.

This book goes far beyond its helpful analysis of cultural change. It opens up for us two major arenas that touch the heart of the church's work in this new era. First, the immense hunger for authentic spirituality is a mark of our times. Where previous generations flaunted a narrow secular veneer, the people of the postmodern world seem drawn irresistibly to find sources of meaning and transcendance. Nash may be right that we are in—or on the edge of—a period as rich as the Great Awakening. He sees, as all of us do, masses of inchoate signs of hunger for the spiritually authentic behind the attraction to any kind of group or fad that touches otherworldly dimensions.

Yet this hunger for spirituality does not today, perhaps for the first time in many centuries, cause people to come to the churches. Somehow by the way churches are articulating their message and living it out, they are not communicating that authentic spirtuality is to be found there. If Nash is right, that we live in the midst of a time of genuine spiritual search analogous to the Great Awakening, how do we communicate the riches of our spiritual heritage to a generation not interested in being in communication with what churches do? I think Nash is calling us to be a church whose life is transparent to spiritual power and consequently magnetic for those who seek genuine spirituality.

That is the depth of the challenge Nash leads us into. The ways we have been doing our thing have left us out of touch with the very people for whom we hold this treasure of spiritual riches. Questioning, searching people look to the church and do not see spiritual authenticity. The call, then, that I hear Nash helping with is the call to understand the questioning character of our culture and to reframe the ancient message of the gospel so that it can be seen and experienced in the thought-forms of the postmodern culture.

As Nash opens our eyes to the spiritual awakening going on around us, he also lifts up the intense and far-flung desire of the people of today to "make a difference." We who are Christians cannot think about such a statement without articulating it as the calling of almighty God to each of God's children, a call to give themselves to others, to become servants. The desire to "make a difference" is a reflection of one's vocation to follow the way of Christ.

Nash offers us, then, a challenging future for the church: that it would learn to live in the postmodern world and to be unafraid of its challenges, that it open itself to new ways to experience and articulate the timeless truth of the gospel, and that it have the courage to let go of structures of the past, trusting the Lord to lead us to the structures we will need for our ministry in the future.

This book encourages and calls me as I hope it does you. It speaks of the weariness many of us have felt, from time to time, knowing that we have spent years and years bailing out of a boat, fearing that it was sinking. The work, seen that way, is depressing. This book is a call to a new sense of what we are about. I think Nash wants and offers more of a challenge to us. I think he believes we are called to walk on water. And I believe he's right. What's more, with God, I trust that we shall.

Loren Mead

Notes

[1] See the following books written by Loren Mead, published by the Alban Institute, Bethesda MD: *The Once and Future Church* (1991), *Transforming Congregations for the Future* (1994), and *Five Challenges for the Once and Future Church* (1996).

[2] For background on other paradigmatic changes the church has faced historically in understanding its mission, see David Bosch, *Transforming Mission* (Maryknoll NY: Orbis Books, 1994).

Acknowledgments

This book has been an intensely personal journey for me. It has provided me with the opportunity in the solitude of my own heart and mind to reflect upon the journey of the people of God called the church. But my thoughts have not occurred in a vacuum. In fact, none of them belong to me alone. They were born out of the reflections of many people, all of whom belong to the church and care deeply about it.

First, I must thank the congregations that raised me in the faith or that had enough faith in me to call me as their minister. These congregations span the globe. My "home" church, the Cotabato City Baptist Church on the island of Mindanao in the Philippines, baptized me in 1967, at low tide in the salty water of the Moro Gulf. The First Baptist Church of Milledgeville, Georgia, called me to serve as a summer youth minister in 1978, despite my youth and inexperience. The North Rolling Fork Baptist Church of Gravel Switch, Kentucky, and the Buechel Park Baptist Church of Louisville, Kentucky, called me to be their pastor in 1985 and 1989, respectively. Both churches serve as wonderful models for what the body of Christ ought to be.

I extend my deepest appreciation and thanks to Dr. Bill J. Leonard, my teacher and dear friend, who read this manuscript and encouraged me in the writing process. His ideas have been so profoundly influential upon my own vision for the church that I hardly know where his thoughts end and mine begin. I hope he will forgive any theft.

Two faculty colleagues at Shorter College deserve special thanks. Dr. Steven Sheeley, my good friend and teaching associate, served as a sounding board and critic. His insights and many contributions are gratefully acknowledged. Dr. Wilson Hall, professor of English and German and my kindred spirit in the world of ideas, offered helpful suggestions.

Stephanie McFarland, my research assistant, gathered sources and offered a patient ear as I wrote and rewrote numerous drafts. Melanie Register typed the bibliography and helped in the final frantic days before the deadline. These two students, along with the other religion and

Christian ministry majors at Shorter College, first heard the ideas presented in these pages. As always, I learned from them at least as much as I taught. I am grateful for the community of faith and learning that is nurtured among us.

A word of thanks to Kim Herndon and Karen Simpkins in the Livingston Library at Shorter College for their help in securing source materials. Their assistance with interlibrary loans and other chores certainly made the writing task more pleasant.

I owe a special debt of gratitude to Guyeth, Lindsay, and Douglas Nash. Here words finally fail me. I will do my best to express my love and appreciation in more tangible ways.

Introduction

The Sinking Ship

Salt is good,
but if it no longer
tastes like salt,
how can it be made
to taste salty again?
(Luke 14:34 CEV)

"Daddy, church is boring," my six-year-old son whispered in the middle of a recent worship service. His head rested in my lap, and he stared up at the ceiling with a facial expression that asked, "Must I endure this?"

I looked around. Most congregants obviously agreed with him. A couple of heads nodded. People glanced at their watches.

"Daddy." He tugged at my sleeve. "Are we gonna get to drink Jesus' blood and eat the crackers?"

I suppose that any six-year-old enjoys drinking blood and eating crackers!

"We just did that last week," I said. "We can't do it again for about three months!"

He wrinkled his nose in disgust. "Too bad," he said. "I really like it!"

And I liked it, too! As the service progressed, I wondered why we didn't celebrate communion more often. Did we fear a mystical experience? Did we not want to appear too "Catholic"? I finally concluded that practicality was the major reason behind a quarterly communion service. Communion was simply impractical on a regular basis—it took too much time and required cleanup afterwards.

As I consulted my "order" of worship, it occurred to me that there was little room for spontaneity in the service. Worship began with the organ prelude. Ushers gathered in the offering at the appropriate time. The sermon was delivered in a scholarly fashion by an intelligent and committed pastor. The choir sang just before the sermon.

It occurred to me that a little less practicality and order might help my son (and myself) to enjoy worship a bit more. Children are more honest than the rest of us. Church *is* boring—at least the kinds of churches to which most of us belong! And perhaps it is boring because it is so well-ordered. The "order" of worship is just about the only constant in our lives.

In the last twenty years we Americans have witnessed dramatic changes in the wider culture. We have moved from record albums and 8-track tapes to compact discs, from electric typewriters to Pentium computers, and from board games to SuperNintendo. America's towns and cities have become global communities, with Muslim mosques, Buddhist temples, and New Age bookstores competing with Christian churches for the faith loyalties of the American people.

Yet local churches have hardly changed. The most advanced piece of technology in most children's Sunday School classes is a flannel board. Church bulletins in the 1990s look surprisingly similar to those of the 1950s. Worship is a stagnant and endless litany of hymn after sermon after choral anthem after offering after prayer after hymn after welcome and announcements. Preachers drone on to half-empty sanctuaries, mistakenly assuming that their congregants are even listening at all. People attend out of loyalty to the institution and their own investment in the building rather than because of any real sense of spiritual enhancement.

And we continue to "do church" as if people will endure this kind of tedium forever. We play a little game each week in church called "Let's Pretend." We pretend that people want the same things from church in the 1990s that they wanted in the 1950s. We pretend that the majority of Americans are churchgoing Christians who believe in the God of the Bible and who order their lives to reflect this reality. We pretend that the spirituality of Americans in the 1990s is enhanced by a decades-old diet of practical faith, old-time religion, revivals, and personal "quiet time." We pretend that the church is still the center of community life and that people will come back to church "when they get their lives straightened out."

For this reason, Christianity in America in the late twentieth century is deeply troubled. The church has three primary responsibilities: to . . .

- offer the truth of God's grace and love to its culture
- enhance the spirituality of its members
- cultivate a caring community that reflects the coming kingdom of God

As the nation has changed, however, the church has failed in these responsibilities. As the culture has become increasingly pluralistic, the church has become embroiled in its own internal war over truth and has failed to extend God's grace and love in a redemptive fashion. A tragic church war between traditionalists and progressivists has robbed the church of its spiritual energy and destroyed its communal witness to that grace and love. The church risks becoming increasingly irrelevant to its culture if it cannot overcome this division.

As the culture has become increasingly interested in spirituality, the church has become highly rational and propositional in its approach to faith. It has defined spirituality as "that body of truth that must be believed." Spirituality has been reduced to the rote memorization of scripture and the defense of propositional truths about God. God is to be obeyed, not experienced.

And, as the culture has changed its notions about community and family in a technological age, the church has continued to insist upon old patterns of community relationships. It has incorrectly assumed that the children who are raised in its walls will adopt the Christian faith for themselves. It has refused to search out new patterns of community that might enhance its ability to minister in its context. It has failed to reflect the kind of community that will exist in the future kingdom of God.

Three recent experiences in my own life have caused me to reflect upon these changing notions about truth, spirituality, and community in American life. These learning experiences occurred in the most unexpected moments and in the most unlikely places—namely in a conversation at the college where I teach, during a book-buying trip to Waldenbooks, and while shopping at Super Wal-Mart. They became launching pads for my own reflections on the church's inability to meet its primary obligations in the twenty-first century.

A Lesson about Truth

The first such experience occurred as I was walking down a hall at the college where I teach.

"Can I ask you a question?" said a voice behind me.

I turned to find a student whom I knew to be a devout Christian with a bright intellect.

"Ask away!" I said, wondering what unanswerable theological riddle might be about to rear its ugly head.

"Do you really believe that Christianity is the only true religion?"

I stopped dead in my tracks.

She went on. "You know that I'm a Christian. But I can't believe that Christianity is the only path to God. I know too many people—Jews and Buddhists especially—who follow a different faith. How can I tell them that their faith, their truth, is less valid than mine?"

Her question disturbed me. I thought about the assumptions that rested behind it—that truth was relative, that more than one religion might be "true." I thought about the increasing numbers of students raised in good Baptist, Methodist, or Catholic homes who ask similar questions:

• "Isn't it arrogant to believe that my faith is the only true faith?"
• "Am I still a Christian if I practice yoga and believe in reincarnation?"
• "Is there a single Power behind all religions?"

A Lesson about Spirituality

Another experience occurred a couple of years ago on a visit to Walden-books in the local mall. A friend had asked if I had any good books on angels. Billy Graham's *Angels* came to mind, but I wanted to check for something a little more recent.

"What books do you carry on angels?" I asked.

The salesclerk nearly doubled over with laughter.

"I only have about a hundred," he replied. And he took me to the "religion" section. Books on angels covered a full bookcase from top to bottom. I was stunned. My eyes scanned the titles:

4

- *Ask Your Angels: A Practical Guide to Working with the Messengers of Heaven to Enrich Your Life* by Alma Daniel
- *A Book of Angels* by Sophy Burnham
- *Angels: the Mysterious Messengers* edited by Rex Hauck
- *An Alphabet of Angels* by Nancy Willard
- *An Angel to Watch Over Me* by Joan Wester Anderson
- *The Angels Within Us* by John Randolph Price

I thought back fifteen years to my own college days in the late 1970s when I couldn't convince people to believe in God, much less angels!

"Do these books sell?" I asked the clerk.

"Like hot cakes!" he replied.

A Lesson about Community

The final experience occurred on my first visit to a Super Wal-Mart. I was genuinely excited. A kind, gray-haired gentleman handed me a cart and welcomed me to the place, just as if it were some mom-and-pop grocery store in small-town America. Wow, what a store!

I saw a barbershop, a bank, a cleaners, a photo studio, a post office, a pharmacy, a video store, a restaurant, a bakery, a delicatessen, an automobile repair shop, a shoe repair shop, a hardware store, a toy store, a bookstore, a grocery store, a jewelry store, and a dime store—all rolled into one!

"Honey," I cried with delight to my wife, "We don't ever have to shop anywhere else."

I grabbed a child and a cart and headed in one direction, and she grabbed a child and a cart and went in another. I quickly lost my bearings. The aisles were narrow and crammed with people. I looked for a clothes hamper in housewares; it was in home furnishings. The salesperson in home furnishings told me that metal bookends were in books and cards; books and cards told me to look in hardware. Hardware sent me to home furnishings where the whole fiasco had begun. The very same salesperson said, without apology, "Oh, that's right, we don't carry those anymore!"

The man in school supplies barely spoke English. "Where are the mops?" I asked.

"You want paper mop or book mop?" he queried.

I looked at him with a puzzled expression on my face.

He responded with considerable disdain, as if I were a tourist asking a stupid question. "You want mop of Alabama or mop of Georgia or all mops together?" He then started helping a nice Muslim couple dressed in traditional Islamic garb.

I tried to buy a phone and answering machine in electronics. "Yes, sir," said the young computer whiz who worked there. "Would you like a speakerphone with that or remote capability, and would you prefer a digital or tape system, and how many numbers do you want to put in the memory for speed dialing, and would you like it to repeat the day and time for your convenience? And what about a hold button or mute button or redial button? And do you need a room monitor or memo recording, or what about two-way recording?"

My wife found me on some dark, forgotten aisle babbling away incoherently. My cart was empty. My daughter had disappeared. We found her in electronics playing SuperNintendo with the clerk. It was obvious that she was in her element—though I was certainly not in mine. After taking four Advil, I vowed never to darken the door of a Super Wal-Mart again. I have broken my vow. Everyone goes to Super Wal-Mart !

A New Reality

Now at first glance, a conversation with a college student, a visit to Waldenbooks, and a trip to Super Wal-Mart seem unrelated. But I am convinced that they have much in common. They have become parables for me that speak volumes about cultural and religious realities in late twentieth-century American life, realities with which previous generations of Americans have never had to deal.

My conversation with the young student at a Baptist college caused me to reflect on the ways in which our understanding of absolute truth has changed. Once upon a time, people rarely questioned the validity of the Christian faith. In fact, the American nation was dominated by the Christian worldview. Methodists, Presbyterians, and Baptists got along well despite their differences. They shared a common understanding of reality that said that the world was created by the God of Jesus Christ. Americans shared common Christian notions about morality, the divine destiny of the nation, and the afterlife.

Certainly there were some differences. On occasion, a Methodist might even marry a Baptist (or vice versa). But she (or he) never joined the Baptist church. To be immersed was to deny one's heritage. Differences were important, but we all shared a common faith.

Today that common faith is crumbling. New religions have captured the faith loyalties of Americans. And the introduction of those new religions has raised new doubts about the validity of any single religion, including Christianity. Now only one in every four Americans believes in an absolute truth.

My experience at Waldenbooks is a parable of the way Americans have become increasingly interested in issues of spirituality. Books on angels, Eastern religions, meditation, and self-improvement reflect a culture-wide interest in such matters. In the past, spirituality in America was uniquely Christian in its expression. Most Americans looked to the church as the spiritual center for the nation. Some churches had a gauge in the Sunday School room called the "offering envelope." A checklist was written on it! You got twenty points for each category—Bible Brought, Bible Read Daily, Lesson Studied, Giving, Worship Attendance. I usually vacillated between 60 and 80 percent. I was a good kid!

Today Americans pick up books on angels and meditation with little regard for the source of this spirituality. A spiritual revolution is quietly taking place just outside the church walls. For the first time in our national history, that revolution has little to do with the church. People treat religions like winter coats they can put on or take off depending on changes in the weather. They dabble for awhile in a Baptist or Methodist church, check out Presbyterianism or Catholicism, and experiment with Eastern forms of meditation. In the process, Christianity is quickly being marginalized as merely one among a number of religious perspectives.

And my "Super Wal-Mart" experience brought to my attention the dramatic changes in community patterns that Americans have experienced in the last fifty years. Life used to be simple. Few choices existed. Americans shopped in the town square or along Main Street. Grocery stores sold food, and hardware stores sold hardware. You couldn't buy hammers and pork chops at the same place! We drove Fords or Chevys. We read *Time* or *Newsweek*. We watched ABC, NBC, or CBS. The President generally received our respect, if not our blind trust. We sat on our porches, borrowed eggs from our neighbor, and raised her children along with our own. Today we often cannot recall our neighbor's name.

The America we once knew is now gasping for its last breath! That old world was quite comfortable for the church. The church was made for it! We knew the boundaries! Baptist, Methodist, post office, drugstore, white, black, Jewish, Catholic, Protestant, Republican, Democrat, ABC, the NFL on CBS (no one had ever heard of FOX), church, world, Christian, non-Christian, faith, science—everything was in its place. The only religion on TV consisted of those quartet singers who pumped you up for church on Sunday morning. Muslims lived in the Middle East, and Buddhists never strayed much past California. Everyone colored within the lines!

Now the colors are running together. Consider the following:

- The PTO president at the elementary school my children attend opened a recent meeting with a devotional reading from *A Cherokee Feast of Days*, a book about Native American spirituality.
- The first two Muslim chaplains were recently appointed for ministry to U. S. military personnel.
- The Buddhist Churches of America now include some sixty independent churches and forty branches scattered from California to New York. Their Sunday School department publishes study guides, lessons, and children's books for use in local Buddhist churches.
- A recent commercial on television portrayed a "politically correct" football locker room in which a line of priests and preachers and monks and baghwans offered a prayer for the team.
- Mainline Protestant churches continue to decline in membership. Young adults are leaving the church in record numbers, convinced that there are other pathways to a successful and meaningful life than that offered by Christianity.
- People talk today of a post-Christian world in which the church no longer dominates the cultural scene.

The Sinking Ship

These changes are symptoms of a profound national cultural transformation brought on by technological advances, global shrinking, and increasing pluralism. And this cultural transformation presents a great challenge to Christian faith. The church runs scared. As the ship sinks, some passengers throw excess baggage overboard—Sunday night services, orders of worship, outdated music, week-long revivals, an older minister who can't "appeal to young people"—all of these go splashing into the water below in an effort to keep the boat afloat.

Other passengers cry out for new equipment—new sanctuaries, family life centers, praise choruses on overhead projectors, spiritual retreats—anything that might give the old ship an overhaul. A few passengers throw everything out and re-outfit the whole ship. They even scratch off the name of the owner and refer to it as "The Lighthouse Church" or "The Gathering."

And for some ships, these efforts seem to work. Passengers stay on board. New passengers sign on. But for most captains and crew, the best they can do is to bail water out the back as quickly as it comes in the front. The church remains somewhat stable. But it lives with the reality that eventually it will sink.

Why am I writing this book? I write it because I have stood in the boat and bailed water for at least seventeen years. I have pastored three churches and served as a youth minister, an associate pastor, a deacon, and a church member. Now I teach at a Baptist college where religion majors are preparing for Christian ministry. I feel an obligation to be honest with them about the state of the church as it approaches the twenty-first century. And I feel compelled to wrestle with the challenges that the church faces and to offer some vision for the church in a new era in which Christianity is not the only faith in town.

I also write this book for church members and clergy who minister in what I call "traditional churches." These churches are composed of people who sit in the same pew Sunday after Sunday and enjoy "beating the Methodists" to the steakhouse for Sunday dinner. They prefer traditional music in worship, enjoy a good revival now and then, and believe that "Thou shalt have church on Sunday night" is the eleventh commandment. They observe communion exactly once a quarter! These folks know that church is boring and, when pressed, would admit that they

9

prefer for it to stay that way forever! They are good, salt-of-the earth people for whom church has become a way of life.

My purpose is twofold. First, I want to help ministers and concerned church members in these traditional churches make sense of a changing world. Walter Truett Anderson has said that "reality isn't what it used to be."[1] He is absolutely right. The nation has undergone dramatic change since the decade of the 1950s. A new reality now exists that the church must understand if it is to influence its surrounding culture.

My second purpose is to assist traditional churches in developing a vision for ministry in the twenty-first century that takes seriously this cultural transformation. Christian clergy and laity alike are scratching their heads in bewilderment over how to minister in such a rapidly changing culture. We must remember that the church has survived for some two thousand years because it has retained a chameleon-like ability to change its structures and appearance when necessary in order to offer the truth of God's grace and love to its culture, revitalize its spirituality, and provide a community of faith for its membership.

One needs only to look back to Christian history for proof of the necessity of this constant realignment. The early church, threatened with extinction by the Roman persecutions, transformed the murder of Christians into a symbol of the victory of God over the forces of evil. The medieval church, virtually paralyzed by its own corruption, recovered the centrality of scripture, grace, and faith as the primary means of salvation. And the American church, sharply divided along ethnic and religious lines, utilized revivalism and denominationalism as the means by which to enliven the faith of frontier settlers and to unite and evangelize the nation.

I firmly believe that the church must "re-form" itself once again if it is to meet the spiritual challenges of American life in the twenty-first century. You probably agree with me, or you would not be reading this book! Such reformation will require far more than a shift from hymnbooks to praise choruses on overhead projectors. It will not be cured by one-day spiritual retreats that replace week-long revivals. Rather, it necessitates a complete overhaul of our notions about what it means to be "church."

This book suggests that cultural changes in American life can be traced to a philosophical reality known as "postmodernity" that even

10

traditional churches must understand. Postmodernity will serve as the cultural context in which the church will operate in the twenty-first century. Already, postmodern Americans are making dramatic, new assumptions about truth, spirituality, and the nature of community. The church must take seriously "postmodern" understandings of these essential categories if it is to revitalize itself for ministry in this new day.

The first chapter traces the cultural transition in American life from "modernity" to "postmodernity." Why has this change occurred? Why should traditional churches bother to understand it? How does it explain the new notions about spirituality, truth, and community that are reflected in my own experiences at a Baptist college, at Waldenbooks, and at Super Wal-Mart?

The second chapter explores the challenges that confront the church as it offers the truth of God's grace and love in a postmodern world. The church's undying allegiance to rational, intellectual, and unemotional worship now hinders its witness to the truth of the Christian faith. In the modern world, Christianity provided the central faith story of the American people. In a postmodern world, it now finds itself on the margins competing with other religions for the faith-loyalty of its culture.

This marginalization has created a devastating culture war within the church between traditionalists and progressivists who offer radically different solutions to the problem. "Traditionalists" whistle into the winds of change, insisting that everyone accept a single, absolute truth. "Progressivists" advocate an open, accepting toleration of other worldviews, thus risking the truth-claims of Christianity on the altar of pluralism. These two groups are engaged in a battle to determine the future of the American nation. What is the role of the church in this great battle? Is its role to preserve truth, as the traditionalists would argue? Or should the progressivist vision of tolerance and openness prevail?

The third and fourth chapters offer some solutions to this dilemma. The third chapter is concerned with the church's responsibility to enhance the spiritual vitality of its membership. Here I explore the ways in which a postmodern worldview has caused a recent outbreak of spirituality in America and an interest in all forms of religion. At the same time, the culture war between traditionalist and progressivist Christians has sapped the spiritual energy of Christian churches. In such an environment, the church, and particularly traditional churches, has been marginalized. What can the church do in an age of meditation, scented candles, and crystals to revitalize its own spirituality and to overcome the devastating influence of the culture war?

The fourth chapter explores changing patterns of community in postmodern America. In the past, Americans viewed church as the center of community life. Today we go where we can get the kind of religion we want, quickly, and with the least amount of trouble. Other organizations compete with the church for the attention of its constituents. Lines between denominations are quickly fading. What kind of community should the church become in the twenty-first century? What will people want? What will God expect?

The conclusion calls for a renewed vision for what it means to be a traditional church in the twenty-first century. This vision will take seriously the perceptions about absolute truth, spirituality, and Christian community that dominate in a postmodern America. It will look back to the early church as a model for ministry in a pluralistic age. And it will encourage traditional churches to look to sister churches in Asia, Africa, and South and Central America as sources for spiritual and communal renewal.

Note

[1]See Walter Truett Anderson, *Reality Isn't What It Used to Be: Theatrical Politics, Ready-to-Wear Religion, Global Myths, Primitive Chic, and Other Wonders of the Postmodern World* (San Francisco: HarperSanFrancisco, 1990).

Chapter 1

The Worlds

*No one pours new wine
into old wineskins.
The wine would swell
and burst the skins.*
(Matt 9:17 CEV)

Our first task is to try to understand such terms as premodernity, modernity, and postmodernity. Don't let these philosophical concepts get the best of you! They refer to particular stages in human history. The premodern age emerged with the earliest human civilizations and lasted well into the seventeenth century. The modern age was inaugurated in the late seventeenth and early eighteenth century with a renewed emphasis upon human reason and science. And the postmodern world has emerged in the last thirty years as the limitations of science and rationalism have become increasingly evident and a rebirth of religion has occurred.

I want to explain how the church has been influenced by the ideas about God that emerged in each of these three periods of human history. Understanding such influences will enable us to see how Christian ministry should change to meet the spiritual needs of our own day.

Premodernity
Beginnings of Recorded History to 1700

Premodern human beings believed that the universe was the playground of the gods or God. Life was beyond human control and could be explained only in supernatural terms. Natural disasters and illness were interpreted as signs of divine displeasure. Chaos reigned in the universe. The only way to bring order to human existence was to befriend or placate the gods, thus ensuring their cooperation in battling the evil and the chaos.

The church existed within this premodern worldview through its first seventeen centuries. The early church was born into a pluralistic context in which various religions sought to explain reality and to offer hope and solace to their constituents. Christianity gained the upper hand among the various religions of the Roman empire when Emperor Constantine came to power in the fourth century. The Christian and premodern worldview then became the dominant lens through which the Western world perceived its reality.

The idea of God's absolute power and authority over all of human life formed the foundation for the premodern Christian worldview. Augustine of Hippo championed the notion that God reigned supreme over both church and state. The state existed for the purpose of enforcing the moral structures of society. And the church existed to ensure the salvation of souls.

The culture of the Middle Ages was thus a uniquely religious culture in which God was intimately involved in every facet of human experience. Medieval Christians placated God by purchasing and viewing relics, going on pilgrimages, and attending mass. To fail to please God or the church was to put both one's life and one's soul in jeopardy. God visited pestilence, disease, and damnation upon the wicked!

Modernity
1600–1960

Then modernity set in. As the Renaissance unfolded in the seventeenth century, humankind toppled God from the throne of cultural, theological, and philosophical domination, placing itself at the center of the universe. The church no longer controlled the boundaries of human knowledge, even knowledge about God. Human beings recovered some sense of their own power to effect change in the world. The human mind was applied to such problems as politics, education, law, and the nature of war. God was still very important. But God had provided human beings with minds that should be utilized for the good of the human race.

At this same time, significant scientific discoveries shattered long-held ideas about the universe itself. Copernicus and Galileo proved that the earth was not the center of the universe. The church immediately condemned such views, pitting itself against the emerging scientific community and creating a conflict from which it has yet to recover. When Isaac Newton and others established that the universe operated according to certain well-established laws, the church was dethroned as the chief link between God and humanity. Human beings could depend upon these natural laws. And God, though highly respected for having established the rules, was no longer feared as a capricious deity who might at any time destroy the ungodly.

The Enlightenment finished off what the Renaissance and the scientific revolution had begun. René Descartes, the philosophical father of modernity, set himself to the task of doubt. He doubted every single thing he had ever known in a grand effort to uncover the one thing that could not be doubted. He concluded that the doubting mind itself was that single undoubtable thing and that human reason was the only credible path to knowledge.

Since Descartes, modernists have applied human reason to the discovery of the natural laws that govern the universe. The chief characteristic of the modern age is its supreme confidence in the human mind. In such an environment, science reigns supreme. God stands on the sidelines as the referee who started the game, but whose only role now is to ensure that no rules are broken.

The church has existed within this modern worldview for almost three centuries. It is essentially the water in which the church swims. Like the churchgoing people of medieval Europe who were immersed in a premodern worldview, we assume that our modern view is the true picture of reality. Nothing will be accepted unless it is first proven according to the dictates of science.

The Bible itself falls victim to this over-emphasis upon human reason. It is viewed as an inerrant, infallible prooftext for reality. Complicated formulas are utilized to show that the Bible makes rational sense. I remember a visit by a nuclear physicist to a Baptist Student Union meeting during my college days. This scientist impressed upon us his firm conviction that the Bible was a rational and scientific document even though it had been written in a prescientific age. He argued that its authority as God's Word was proven by the fact that it contained medical knowledge that was centuries ahead of its time. I remember how impressed I was by this rational defense of the Bible. Such tactics were undertaken in order to combat such scientific theories as evolution and the "big bang."

The doctrines of the church are similarly affected by the modern age. In the late 1970s I read Josh McDowell's *Evidence that Demands a Verdict* in which McDowell articulates a rational defense of Jesus' divinity.[1] Using an argument first expressed in the Middle Ages, McDowell says that three responses can be made to the life of Jesus. Either Jesus is Lord, a liar, or a lunatic. And he points out that many of Jesus' followers died for their firm conviction regarding Jesus' divinity.

The proof of that divinity then rests in the fact that rational human beings such as the disciples accepted it without question. They would not die for a lie; neither would they follow a crazed lunatic. McDowell's point is that we rational human beings of the twentieth century should then also accept Christ's divinity as a trustworthy foundation for Christian faith. By buying into such rational interpretations, the church has admitted that science and rationalism are the criteria by which reality should be judged.

I recently led a devotional for a youth group. One young woman, tired of the dissonance between her high school education and her faith, exclaimed, "Why is it that we are taught one thing at school and another thing at church, and, to be perfectly honest, the things we learn at school make a lot more sense?" She is absolutely right. Science will always win the battle against religion on the playing field of human reason. In a rational age, Christianity is relegated to the sidelines. This marginalization is hardly avoidable. After all, Christianity emerged in a premodern era when miracles and healings were not subjected to the scientific method. Resurrection is easily defended in a premodern age, but hardly believable in the modern world, at least according to the dictates of science.

Postmodernity
1960–present

My, how times have changed! The modern world, with its emphasis upon human reason and its devaluation of religious faith, is in a steep decline. I recently attended an office party at an exclusive Atlanta hotel as the guest of my wife's employer, an outplacement consulting firm. We milled around the food tables, chatting with the partygoers. Slightly uncomfortable in the "corporate" environment, I tried to be as inconspicuous as possible, assuming that most attendees would find a religion professor to be rather bland company.

In fact, I quickly became the center of attention! One woman asked my opinion of the idea of reincarnation, a belief she had recently adopted. A distinguished-looking and well-tanned middle-aged man informed me that he led wholistic health seminars on cruise ships. The three of us engaged in a rather animated discussion about the search for meaning in life. Both persons seemed vitally interested in the Christian faith as it had shaped my own life. What did I find valuable about it? Did it offer an adequate spirituality for me?

I was struck by the direction of the conversation. None of us raised the question of the reasonableness of our belief systems. Rational justifications for our religious perspectives seemed hardly worth discussing! We talked about how our respective views on resurrection, reincarnation, and wholistic medicine provided meaning for our lives. Such a discussion would have seemed hardly imaginable ten years ago, especially in a corporate environment where people usually avoided the topic of religious faith.

No one is quite sure exactly when postmodernity replaced modernity as the dominant worldview of the American people. Many scholars tie its demise to the growing awareness of the limitations of science and rationalism that gradually emerged through the twentieth century. Such historic events as World Wars I and II, Hiroshima and Nagasaki, the Nazi Holocaust, and Chernobyl have contributed to the notion that the human mind alone cannot solve the world's problems. At the same time, religious and political worldviews have collided as transportation and communication methods have improved. This collision, which reached a crisis point in the 1960s, raised doubts about the existence of a single religious truth or worldview that could explain the universe.

This new openness to the faith perspectives of other people signaled a radical transition in American culture, namely the movement from modernity to postmodernity. The cultural dissonance of the 1960s caused a reevaluation of the direction of the modern world. In what turned out to be modernity's last gasp, scientists and philosophers proclaimed the death of God, insisting that science and rationalism had triumphed over religious faith. Ironically, the exact opposite was true. It was science that had "outlived its usefulness."[2] And today scientists themselves are castigating science for its "appalling spiritual damage" and its elevation of human reason at the expense of religious faith.[3]

Many Americans now believe that scientific truth about the world may not be the only truth. Science has its limitations. While the accomplishments of science bordered on the miraculous—placing a man on the moon, discovering cures for polio and other terrible diseases, and harnessing the power of the atom—science failed to explain the ultimate questions of human existence. It told us how we came to be, but not why we came to be.

Suddenly, Americans are searching for answers to the questions that science has failed to answer. We are again interested in the supernatural—in reincarnation and resurrection, in angels and demons, in healing and miracles. We want to rediscover the supernatural.

But the church has been caught flat-footed by this spiritual resurgence. It still swims in the fishbowl of modernity. Traditional churches advocate a carefully constructed and rational system of belief based upon a scientifically verifiable Bible. Worship is well-ordered and devoid of spontaneity. Sunday School teachers defend the faith against science. The focus of church is on force-feeding propositional truths about God to an American public that is crying out for an experience with God.

Conclusion

The church has three primary obligations:

• to offer the truth of God's grace and love to its culture
• to enhance the spiritual lives of its members
• to provide a place of community that reflects the kingdom of God

These obligations did not change for the church when the premodern world gave way to the modern world. They remain the same even in the midst of the transition from modernity to postmodernity.

The ways in which these obligations are met *must* change, however. Herein lies the problem for most ministers and church members who recognize that "church is boring" and are desperately trying to sound a warning. Too many churches have confused the primary obligations of the church with the secondary means by which the church accomplishes those obligations. Thus it has always been. Churches confuse style with substance.

As the sixteenth century dawned, there were only two branches of the church, one in the West and one in the East. No one had ever held a week-long revival. Nor had they ever heard the word "denomination." Church didn't necessarily happen at eleven o'clock on Sunday morning and at seven o'clock on Sunday night. Communion was a weekly affair! Preachers never married. The first Protestant foreign missionary would not be born for another 150 years.

Imagine now that you are a time traveler. You climb into your time machine and travel back to Rome, Italy, in the year 1510. Once there, you make an appointment with Pope Julius II to encourage him to make some needed reforms in the church so that Christianity is not divided into hundreds of denomination. You describe to him the church of the future. You warn him about an Augustinian monk in Germany named Martin Luther.

You talk about the new churches and denominations that will be formed over the next hundred years—the Lutheran church in Germany, the Reformed church in Switzerland, Anabaptist churches in Switzerland and Holland, the Church of England. You try to describe the various theologies that will emerge and the different kinds of worship styles. You talk of religious freedom and the separation of church and state. The pope pays you no attention. How can you blame him? No one in 1510 could ever have imagined that such vast change was about to shake the medieval church to its very foundations.

Why did such change occur? The church neglected its obligations. It ignored its own spiritual corruption. It offered empty ritual, not meaningful worship. It reflected its culture instead of transforming it. It assumed that its constituents would remain loyal despite its shortcomings.

So it is with the church of Jesus Christ in the late twentieth century. It is time for traditional churches to sit up and take notice. How can we meet our obligations in a new day? Can we envision new ways to carry the truth of God's grace and love to a world that refuses to accept any single truth as absolute? Can we revitalize and enhance the forms of spirituality in which most of us were raised? And what new kind of community should we become in the twenty-first century?

Notes

[1]Josh McDowell, *Evidence that Demands a Verdict: Historical Evidences for the Christian Faith* (San Bernardino CA: Here's Life Publishers, 1979).

[2]John Horgan, *The End of Science: Facing the Limits of Knowledge in the Twilight of the Scientific Age* (Reading MA: Helix Books, 1996) 6.

[3]Bryan Appleyard, *Understanding the Present: Science and the Soul of Modern Man* (New York: Doubleday, 1993).

Chapter 2

The Wall

Christ has made peace.
He has united us
by breaking down
the wall of hatred
which separated us.
(Eph 2:14 CEV)

During a recent Sunday afternoon walk, my family and I chanced upon some neighbors who had recently moved to our city. When I identified myself as a religion professor at a Baptist college, the husband exclaimed, "Wonderful! We're trying to find a good church here. Can you point us toward one?"

"Which denomination do you prefer?" I asked.

"We don't really care about 'denomination,' " said his wife, bracketing the last word in quotation marks with her fingers as if it were some four-letter obscenity. "We're looking for a pro-life church that teaches the Bible."

Her meaning was obvious. She desired for her family an affiliation with a particular kind of church—a "Bible-believing" church that held to a common set of moral and theological assumptions. She hoped to associate with other Christians who would support her ethical and theological positions on such issues as abortion, prayers in school, capital punishment, and private school vouchers. She did not care whether that church was Baptist or Methodist or Episcopalian. And she certainly wanted to avoid certain "other" kinds of churches—i.e. "pro-choice churches that do not believe the Bible."

Our conversation drew my attention to a disturbing reality that confronts the church at the end of the twentieth century. James Hunter's recent classic, *Culture Wars: The Battle to Define America,* points out that American culture now finds itself caught in a great cultural divide between traditionalists and progressivists.[1] The church has quickly gotten caught up in the battle as traditionalist Christians, consisting mainly of fundamentalists and conservatives, have declared war against moderate to liberal Christians who belong to the progressivist camp.

On the traditionalist side, political and religious conservatives call for a return to "traditional values" and to the moral and religious heritage of Judaism and Christianity. Traditionalist Christians such as my neighbors trace the nation's troubles to a loss of confidence in transcendent authority, namely the Bible, and to its lack of faith in God. For them, the Bible is the unchanging Word of God that transcends time and space and whose teachings can be applied quite legalistically and arbitrarily in any context.

On the progressivist side, political and religious moderates and liberals call for toleration and for the accommodation of the Christian faith to an increasingly pluralistic world. Progressivist Christians believe that the Bible is a legitimate source of authority but that it must be reinterpreted in light of the realities of the late twentieth century. Its teachings are not to be applied arbitrarily; rather, Christians are to search out the principles that rest behind its stories and laws and apply those principles to contemporary life. Progressivists thus often arrive at radically different theological and ethical conclusions from those of Christian traditionalists.

Both groups of Christians face quite a dilemma. Christianity is an exclusive faith that, for hundreds of years, has claimed to possess the only true path to God. It is unique among the major world religions in its insistence that human beings must accept its truth-claims in order to attain salvation. This exclusivity has been increasingly questioned in recent years as religious diversity has increased. Traditionalist and progressivist Christians have responded quite differently to this threat.

Traditionalists, sensing a loss of place and power for themselves as well as for the nation, have called for the recovery of the old biblical culture that dominated in a bygone era. They believe that truth is to be found in the historic Christian propositions about God that emerge from the Scriptures. They insist that correct belief is the single essential element the church must protect. They are quite optimistic about the human ability to discern such truth in the Bible and through divine revelation.

Progressivists are quite the opposite. They preach tolerance and openness and are pessimistic about the human ability to grasp ultimate truth. While they do believe that ultimate truth exists and that it is to be found in the Christian faith, they also believe that no human being can possess it. Therefore, the progressivist search for truth requires an openness to other perspectives. Progressivists insist that Christian love is the single essential element the church must not sacrifice.

Traditionalists and progressivists engage in politically-charged rhetoric in order to promote their particular visions for the Christian faith. Traditionalists charge progressivists with being liberals who support abortion and oppose prayer in public schools. Progressivists counter that traditionalists are fundamentalist reactionaries and racists who favor the legislation of their own particular brand of Christian morality.

I witnessed an exchange between a traditionalist and a progressivist Christian on a college campus shortly after Bill Clinton's 1992 election victory. The progressivist, a college professor, stopped the traditionalist, an administrator, in the hallway:

"What did you think about the election?" asked the progressivist.

"I feel like we just committed a grave national sin by putting an abortionist in the White House," the traditionalist responded.

"You do?" said the progressivist. And with undisguised glee he added, "I feel like we just recommitted our national life to Jesus Christ by kicking out a racist Republican."

This debate has opened up a dividing line within American Christianity that cuts across denominational lines. American religious life has fragmented. Methodists, Baptists, Presbyterians, and Catholics now find themselves divided, not by theological distinctiveness, but rather by the culture war between traditionalists and progressivists. John Simpson put it this way:

> Increasingly, fundamentalist, evangelical, and conservative Christians realized that the real enemy was not the Roman Catholic or the Jew, but the smiling, flexible, civil Protestant modernist.[2]

Let me borrow a metaphor from David Spangler, a New Age spokesperson and critic, to describe the transition that has occurred.[3] Throughout most of its history, American Christianity has been a kind of massive cathedral with various hallways and altars and chapels. Baptists worshiped in one corner, Methodists in another, and Catholics in yet another. Even Judaism established its own little chapel in the huge church. But we all stood inside the same cathedral. Our basic understanding of truth emerged from a common source, the traditions and trappings of an institutionalized Judeo-Christian heritage.

This great American religious cathedral is being remodeled as a result of the debate between traditionalists and progressivists. The walls between its chapels are slowly being removed, and a single great wall is being built that divides traditionalists in various American denominations from their progressivist counterparts.

What exists today is a diversity of special-interest groups and new religious forms that often divide themselves along traditionalist and progressivist lines. To date, some 800 such groups across the landscape of American Christianity have organized to support such causes as nuclear arms reduction, hunger relief, church-state issues, gender equality, pro-life or pro-choice positions on abortion, and a host of other concerns.[4]

Denominations are becoming much less important as sources of identity to American Christians. Instead, church members are finding increasing satisfaction from a broad range of religious groups that cut across denominational lines. Such groups include Sojourners, Habitat for Humanity, Operation Rescue, People for the American Way, Promise Keepers, Fundamentalists Anonymous, the Coalition for Religious Freedom, the National Federation for Decency, and the National Christian Action Coalition.

These groups allow persons to express their opinions in an environment that does not threaten the stability of their local church. In some cases, churches and denominations that are clearly identified with one side of the culture war are able to speak with one voice to the moral and political issues of the day.

Such is the case with the Southern Baptist Convention, a denomination that has been directly influenced by the destructive force of the culture war between traditionalist and progressivist Christians. Since about 1960, Southern Baptists have been embroiled in a "holy war" over the nature of biblical authority.[5] Traditionalist forces in the denomination have now defeated progressivist Baptists by utilizing the power of the presidency of the Southern Baptist Convention to appoint traditionalist trustees to the denomination's agencies and seminaries.[6] But the devastating implications of the controversy for local Baptist churches are only now coming to light.

For two decades, the spiritual energies of the denomination's pastors, theologians, denominational leaders, and church members have been sapped by this debate over the nature of truth. Progressivist pastors and seminary professors have been forced to guard their words carefully lest they be targeted as closet liberals. Many have spoken their minds and paid the price with forced terminations. Traditionalists have been derided as backwoods "rednecks" who utilized the politics of power to manipulate grass-roots Baptists and seize control of the denomination.

As a result of this conflict and because of other forces in American religious life, Southern Baptist churches are in trouble. A recent study by the Home Mission Board of the Southern Baptist Convention reveals that Southern Baptist churches are experiencing near zero growth. Total membership in the average church increased by one person from 1994–1995. Five baptisms were reported along with five other additions in this same time span.[7] Between 1987 and 1995, the median percentage of gifts contributed by churches through the denomination's Cooperative Program has declined from 7.8 percent to 7 percent. This decline can partially be attributed to the traditionalist and progressivist schism.

I am often invited to address secular audiences at other colleges and universities or at civic functions about the peculiarities of Southern Baptists. People in the wider culture find the conflict amusing. Here are some of their recent questions:

"Is the inability to agree with anybody else an essential requirement for becoming a Baptist?"

"Why do Baptists seem to remain in eternal conflict with each other?"

"Do Southern Baptists not realize how ridiculous their continuing debates and wranglings make them look?"

These questions and the statistical decline of not only Southern Baptists but many other denominations make it clear that the debate between traditionalists and progressivists should greatly concern a church that is charged with the task of extending the truth of God's grace and love to the world. We might ask,

- What has caused these widely differing interpretations of biblical authority?
- What is the nature of the truth the church proclaims?
- How is the truth-bearing task of the church to be carried out when the church itself is torn apart by dissension over the nature of that truth?
- Is there any common ground upon which traditionalist and progressivist Christians can come together to offer a common Christian truth to the world?

The Root Cause
Transition from Modernity to Postmodernity

This American cultural war is caused by the transition from a single Christian and American worldview in the modern period to a multicultural and multireligious worldview in the postmodern era. Traditionalists have insisted that truth can be found only in renewed allegiance to biblical authority. Progressivists have insisted that openness and dialogue with other traditions offer the best path for the effective communication of Christian love. Both responses emerge out of a context in which neither side really knows how to share best the Christian faith or maintain the viability of that faith in the face of increasing diversity.

The Search for Truth in the Modern World

The basic tenet of modernity is that a single truth exists and that human beings are engaged in a journey to discover that single truth. In the modern world, the Christian faith and the human mind provided the logical starting places for the search for truth. Christianity pervaded the nation. It was the faith into which most Americans were baptized. From it, they received their basic notions about God, faith, the universe, and the self.

Modern Western philosophy grew up in the shadow of Christianity. Christianity was, after all, the religious environment inhabited by such great champions of the European Enlightenment as René Descartes and David Hume. It was Christianity that was either to be proved or disproved by Enlightenment thinkers as they applied the best tools of rationalism and the scientific method to the faith.

The American nation emerged out of this world of Enlightenment thinking and Christian faith. It possessed a common biblical culture that served as the foundation for the religious worldview of the American people. It was characterized by a uniquely Christian and Protestant view of reality that was fashioned by early English Protestant settlers in the seventeenth century. These settlers brought with them from Europe some common Protestant theological notions about God and church and a mythological understanding of themselves as a chosen people with a divine errand to evangelize the world.

Many other religious traditions either predated this Protestant presence or grew up alongside of it. Native Americans, Catholics, Jews, Mormons, Shakers, Christian Scientists, and a variety of other religious traditions all contributed to the rich mosaic of American religious life and practice. But these traditions were eclipsed in their cultural influence by the power and vitality of American Protestantism and its national vision.

Along with the Christian faith, Americans were also influenced by such Enlightenment categories as rationalism and the scientific method. Just as Protestantism provided the religious framework for the American people, so the European Enlightenment provided the philosophical framework. The modern American nation emerged from the marriage of these two foundational views of reality. The Christian faith served as the cultural umbrella under which most Americans pursued truth. When Americans invoked the name of God, they meant the God of Judaism and Christianity. While the details of how this God operated in the world might be debated, the identity of this God was never in doubt.

This cultural reality enabled the Christian faith to establish itself as the source of the grand story by which most Americans interpreted their lives. This story carried with it the truth about God's relationship with human beings. It asserted that the God of Jesus Christ created the universe and then sent Christ into the world to redeem the creation. It contained certain fixed ideas about God, crucifixion, resurrection, salvation, and the future kingdom of God.

In time, it became inextricably bound to the American story. American Christians believed that their nation was "marked and chosen by the finger of God."[8] Such secular American virtues as materialism, capitalism, and nationalism became intrinsic elements in the story.[9] Mythologies emerged about God's protection of and provision for the American people. The nation's families, schools, and churches became storytellers who preserved the truth of the story and ensured its transmission from generation to generation.

This common Judeo-Christian legacy allowed Will Herberg to pronounce correctly in 1960 that, in the popular American mind, the only true Americans were either Protestants, Catholics, or Jews.[10] Protestantism was the preferred religion of choice, but Judaism and Catholicism were also generally acceptable ways of being religious in America. The church became quite comfortable in such an environment. For Americans, the only acceptable truth was to be found within Christianity or within its parent faith, Judaism. A Judeo-Christian cultural synthesis prevailed in the American nation.

The Search for Truth in a Postmodern World

Then, the decade of the 1960s forever changed the landscape of religion in America. At the beginning of the decade, Americans identified themselves primarily as Protestants, Catholics, and Jews only. By the end of the decade, no one was exactly sure what it meant to be religious in America. Diversity was rampant. The nation's identity underwent a painful process of change.

I was reared in the Philippines in the 1960s as the son of Baptist missionary parents. In that context, Islamic mosques and Hindu funerals were almost as familiar to me as my Sunday School class at the Cotabato City Baptist Church. That early exposure to other religions eventually brought about a crisis in my religious experience as I moved from the childlike faith of my early years to the more mature faith perspective of a young adult.

I was haunted by a single thought: If Christianity is the only true religion, then how can Hindus and Muslims remain so committed to their particular faith traditions? Why can't they see the truth I see? Certainly a few of them did convert to Christianity. But only a very few.

This cosmopolitan environment created a faith crisis for me that the institutional church in the United States now faces. The 1960s signaled a turning point in the nation's religious self-perception that emerged from its subtle exposure to other belief systems. Such exposure has increased almost imperceptibly since that decade as the result of a shrinking globe, technological advancements, and increasing numbers of immigrants from Asia and Africa.

I often jokingly tell my students that the television show "Kung Fu" provided the first sure-fire proof that Americans were well on their way to becoming a postmodern culture. This show, produced in the 1970s, starred David Carradine as a Buddhist monk who utilized his spiritual power to do good in the world. Themes of spirituality had received little attention from television producers prior to the mid-1970s. "Kung Fu" unleashed a new era in television programming that culminated in the 1990s with a myriad of shows devoted to spiritual themes, some of which focused upon Eastern religions.

The years between 1976 and 1996 also unleashed a tidal wave of immigration to the United States, particularly from Asia. I remember the rather shocking experience in 1988 of stopping in east Atlanta on Buford Highway to fill up my car with gas. During my college days in the 1970s I had often stopped at this particular gas station. The surrounding area had been typically suburban, with shopping centers, convenience stores, and fast-food restaurants.

Imagine my surprise when a decade later I discovered that the area had become a center for Asian immigration. Many businesses in the area advertised only in the languages of Chinese, Vietnamese, or Korean. I tried to imagine the havoc this rapid cultural expansion must have caused for area churches.

Technological advancements have also helped to create a multicultural nation. As I write, I am teaching a new course entitled "Global Christianity" that is designed to introduce students to cross-cultural theological issues. The course requires students to correspond by electronic mail with Christian theologians in Africa, Asia, and Central and South America who wrestle daily with the demands of the Christian faith in a non-Western context. Computers are hastening the onset of postmodernity as worldviews collide on a colorful fifteen-inch screen.

In the face of this increasing pluralism, the church has grown increasingly anxious. Thousands of people have left the Christian faith to experiment with other forms of religion. I recently took a class to Birmingham, Alabama, to visit the Birmingham Islamic Society. We were greeted by a former Southern Baptist woman from Oklahoma who had converted to the Islamic faith. In a Birmingham mosque, we watched as three hundred Muslim men prayed to Allah, bowed to Mecca, and were encouraged by their Imam (spiritual leader) to make a pilgrimage to Muhammad's great city.

In such a pluralistic and postmodern world, truth is easily made relative. We might not like such relativization, but, once people have been exposed to many different realities, there really is no going back to the old reality in which a single truth dominates. The very fact that we must defend the old truth provides concrete evidence of the power of competing belief systems. In such an environment, it becomes our responsibility to communicate the truth of Christianity in a world of competing worldviews.

This postmodern context is responsible for the crisis over truth and authority that now confronts the church. Postmodernity has ushered in an era in which many people believe that all realities are socially constructed. In other words, each culture builds its own set of beliefs that determines and orders its reality. In such a system, no single truth exists, and no single authority receives more weight than other authorities.

Postmoderns are quick to point out that cultures adhere to different sets of propositions and accept different authorities. The belief systems that stem from those authorities are "true" for the societies that accept them. In a postmodern world, no single reality can gain the upper hand. Each person is free to pursue whatever reality provides for a meaningful existence.

Consider Walter Truett Anderson's depiction of truth in a postmodern world:

> We all become consumers of reality, . . . and greater numbers of us
> also become creators and merchandisers of reality. As the faith in
> old absolutes wanes, the season opens on the construction of new
> realities for those who do not care to be seen in the standard
> models.[11]

In such a world, no fixed ideas exist or carry enough weight in the culture to be considered the "truth." The postmodern world is a world of competing realities. The stakes are higher. The friendly competition across the street is no longer another Christian tradition. Zen Buddhist centers, New Age bookstores, and Islamic mosques offer radically different realities that are new and exciting and freed from the cultural trappings that often hinder the spiritual vitality of Christianity.

In a postmodern world, knowledge is no longer viewed as an end in itself. Rather, knowledge becomes a commodity that is intended to be sold to the public. We see this quite clearly in political advertising campaigns. Politicians hire image makers who can communicate to the voters a particular worldview. These image-makers then utilize sound-bites, quotes, and statistics to create the impression that the world is a certain way. Political opponents are characterized as soft-on-crime, abortionists, warmongers, or racists.

The voters then buy into or reject this particular view of the world, depending upon whether or not it enables the attainment of their own hopes and dreams. Knowledge is reduced to a commodity because it is nothing more than a means to power. The powerful people are the ones who can most effectively communicate their particular worldview through the media and impose it upon the wider culture. Truth becomes the possession of whatever group holds power. When a new group gains power, the truth changes.[12]

Religious knowledge also becomes a commodity in a postmodern world. Christians insist that the truth-claims of Christianity must be believed. But this insistence upon a single view of truth is largely ignored except by those who choose to accept it. Islam, Buddhism, Hinduism, and other religions offer new worldviews by which Americans may choose to order their realities. In addition, the power of the Christian story is weakened by the fact that Christians cannot agree on the nature of the truth they proclaim. Traditionalist Christians and progressivist Christians serve up what the wider culture views as a commodity, something to be bought into or rejected.

Traditionalist Christians insist upon a fairly common set of theological and ethical issues that they believe to be consistent with the Bible's teachings. John is a traditionalist Christian. He says that the Bible is the

Word of God and that it condemns homosexuality, women pastors, and abortion. He is convinced that he must wage battle to correct these wrongs. So, to that end, he participates in the picketing of abortion clinics. He also refuses to attend any church that allows a woman to serve as a pastor or deacon in the congregation. He vehemently condemns homosexuality, insisting that it is a lifestyle choice and not the result of a person's genetic makeup. He sees AIDS as God's punishment upon homosexuals.

Susan is a progressivist Christian. Her views on the basic moral issues of the day are almost the exact opposite of John's. She is an ordained Baptist minister. She disagrees vehemently with John's position on abortion. She views legalized abortion as an essential right that protects the health of women's bodies and recognizes their full value as human persons. In her estimation, God stands on the side of oppressed women whose rights are being taken away by Operation Rescue and other pro-life advocates. She sees homosexuals as human beings who are to be welcomed and embraced by the church.

Susan and John point accusing fingers at each other. They charge each other with being unchristian or even non-Christian. John insists that true Christians must believe as he does. Susan insists that her perspective is the true Christian perspective. Neither realizes the damage their conflict is causing to Christian faith. Such conflict was damaging enough in a modern world in which Christianity was the only religion for most Americans. But such a conflict becomes exponentially more damaging in a postmodern world in which all truth is viewed as relative truth.

The result of this new and postmodern understanding of truth is the fear, soon to become a reality, that the central story by which most Americans have shaped their reality will be lost. This loss is inevitable. In the future, Christianity will no longer be the sole repository of the faith story of the American people.

We shouldn't be surprised by this eventuality. A single religious faith can never dominate in a nation whose governing documents are based upon the principles of religious liberty and the separation of religion and state. The only religious story that can triumph in such a context is a pluralistic story that celebrates the religious diversity of the American people.

It serves no purpose to protest this turn of events. Most Americans realize that the world has changed. We no longer live in a "Christian America" in which the grand Christian story orders our reality and sustains our cultural vision. That world is dead. It is time to wake up to the new reality, one that insists there is no single Truth but many truths.[13]

More important concerns demand the attention of Christian people. What does this new postmodern reality mean for the church as it seeks to share the truth of God's grace and love in its community? The church must face at least six realities as it prepares for ministry in a post-Christian and postmodern world.

 The grand Christian story has been leveled.

We now play on the same playing field with other great stories. We have no particular advantage. Their truth is as readily acceptable in American culture as our truth. The stories of Hinduism and Buddhism and Mormonism, of New Age religions and goddess worship offer particular views of reality that many Americans find quite meaningful.

We don't like this at all. We cannot understand why sensible and intelligent people would adopt a belief system that is so foreign to that of Christianity. My students often chuckle to themselves when I introduce them to Mormon cosmology with its notions about celestial marriage. I point out that some men in the Mormon tradition will, upon their deaths, be assigned to planets over which they will become gods.

"How can people really believe this?" a student will ask. "It seems so far-fetched!"

I usually respond with what has become my standard answer to such a query. "Hold on just a second. Don't you believe that Almighty God became a man and lived on earth as a man?"

"Yeah!" says the student.

"Then why do you find Mormon theology so difficult to believe?" I ask. "The Mormons have just reversed the process."

Then I go on to help my students see that Christianity is no longer the only reality that is available to the American people. And Christianity cannot compete against other religions by simply chuckling at these belief systems. These other religions are here to stay. People will organize their lives by them. They will believe in them with all of their hearts. And they will make every effort to convince other people that their system is a viable system that can fill life with meaning and purpose.

I believe in the Christian story. I believe with all of my heart that Jesus Christ is Emmanuel—God with us—and that Christ suffered with humanity in his death and overcame death through resurrection. The sin of my broken relationship with God and other human beings is forgiven through Jesus Christ. But I also recognize that these affirmations are simply faith assertions. I have no proof of these truths except the proof I know within my own heart. And I cannot become overconfident that this truth will win the world over simply because I believe it to be the only Truth.

It is this overconfidence that is now seriously hindering the church's witness in the world. Christians sit placidly by, expecting the world to one day grasp the truth. In the meantime, persons of other religious persuasions are about the business of communicating the vitality of their particular faith story.

Several months ago, a student stopped by my office to announce that a Muslim was down in the library talking to people about the Islamic faith.

"We've got to put a stop to it," he said.

"Why?" I asked.

"Because he might win some people over to Islam," he said.

His approach reminded me of the ostrich who hides his head in the sand in order to keep from being seen. It is the response of too many churches to the pluralistic context in which we now live. We ignore other religions, believing that if we ignore them, they will go away. We spend very little time introducing church members to other faith traditions.

Such an approach worked quite well in an environment in which Christianity provided the only spiritual reality for American culture. But it cannot work in a context in which the playing field has been leveled. I recently found a statement that expresses the sentiment of many postmoderns: "He or she who knows only one religion knows no religion." In a postmodern world, we must know the belief systems and stories of other religions.[14] To ignore other religions is to open ourselves up to the charge that we are Christians only because we were born that way. How can we protest this charge with integrity if we have never studied the belief systems of other religious traditions?

Traditionalists and progressivists within the church seem unable to frame a meaningful response to this leveling.

Both Christian traditionalists and Christian progressivists recognize that the church is in serious trouble. Both groups offer solutions that are intended to revitalize the church. But these two groups continue to operate under the umbrella of the Enlightenment and to insist upon modern solutions to a postmodern problem. Bill J. Leonard says that liberal Protestantism (progressivism) and conservative evangelicalism/fundamentalism (traditionalism) are actually "two sides of the same Enlightenment coin."[15]

Both groups emerged in the late nineteenth century as responses to the impact of modernity upon American culture. Modernity challenged Christianity on several levels. The techniques of German higher textual criticism raised questions about the divine inspiration of the Bible. Darwin's theory of natural selection threatened to undermine the creation stories in Genesis. Scientific discoveries raised doubts about the miracles performed in the Bible. Problems of the cities and of industrial expansion only exacerbated the problem. Christian progressives became the champions of intellectual knowledge in such a context, insisting that the Bible should conform to the new scientific discoveries. They sacrificed faith and spirituality on the altar of scientific believability.

Christian traditionalists protected the Bible at all costs, a tactic that has now resulted in the preservation of a spiritless orthodoxy that minimizes spirituality and faith. They insisted that the Bible itself was a scientific textbook that would emerge victorious over the challenges of science. Ironically then, traditionalists caved in to the scientific world, implicitly admitting that science held the key to the successful pursuit of truth.

Two conversations with church members have helped me to see the irrelevancy of this debate between Christian traditionalists and Christian progressivists. About four years ago, an elderly member of my church in Kentucky pulled me aside after a Wednesday night fellowship dinner. "Now, Brother Rob," she said. "My friends keep wanting to know if I am a fundamentalist or a liberal. Which one am I?"

Then on a recent Wednesday night at a church in Georgia, a financial investor in his thirties asked for a few minutes of my time. "I only have about five minutes for this," he said. "But I need a quick summary of the conflict in the Southern Baptist Convention."

I quickly gave him an overview.

When I had finished, he looked at me quizzically and said, "You know, I really don't care one way or the other."

What traditionalists and progressivists fail to understand is that neither group offers an adequate solution to the problem of communicating Christian faith to postmodern people. Both groups have sacrificed the faith on the altar of science. They have caved in to modernity's demand that the Christian faith must be subsumed under the category of science. As a result, traditionalists have wrung the heart out of scripture by insisting that nearly everything in the Bible can be scientifically verified. Progressivists have committed the equally grave sin of tossing anything in the Scriptures that fails to make rational sense.

What can the church do? It must recognize the destructive influences of the conflict between traditionalists and progressivists and move beyond the battle. These two groups remind me of the married couple who found themselves in a terrible argument over what seemed at first to be a vitally important matter. But after hours of arguing, neither party was quite sure what started the struggle. Christianity cannot afford to engage in an internal debate over the nature of truth at the very moment that its culture is growing increasingly suspicious of any claim to absolute truth. To continue the debate only validates the charge that Christians themselves cannot agree on the nature of the truth they proclaim.

All of this is occurring at the very moment that the wider culture is rediscovering faith. People are admitting that science has reached its limits. They are seeking a deeper spiritual reality that can offer meaning to their lives. They are open to truth, any truth, at a time when the church is least prepared to offer that truth to them. Traditionalist Christians and progressivist Christians need to simply look at each other and say, "What are we fighting about anyway? Let's figure out together how to communicate this truth to a world that desperately needs to hear it."

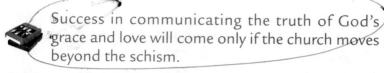

> Success in communicating the truth of God's grace and love will come only if the church moves beyond the schism.

The church must reinvent itself for a postmodern world. It has little choice in the matter. Culture-wide interest in other religions, declining financial support of congregations, and the general loss of Christian power and prestige offer clear evidence of the need for a renewed story. The church must take seriously the specific postmodern context into which it is communicating that story. A multicultural context in which many religions exist together is a far different context than one that is dominated by Christianity alone. Let me illustrate this by returning to Spangler's example of the cathedral.

In the modern world, American Christians met religious seekers at the doorway to the cathedral. These newcomers were invited into the huge building to discover the religious worldview of the American nation. They were enticed into particular rooms of the cathedral by the Methodists or Baptists or Catholics who inhabited those rooms. Theological diversity meant diversity within the Judeo-Christian heritage. People worshiped in a variety of ways. But everyone understood that the great ceiling of the cathedral was formed by a particular religious tradition, that of Judaism and Christianity.

In the postmodern world, the cathedral lies in ruins. It has been destroyed by the popular notion that many kinds of worldviews exist. The cathedral's stones are being carried away one by one. Suddenly, the American religious landscape has become a huge county fair with a limitless sky-blue ceiling, less permanence, and more choices—many of them outside the Christian faith.

In this context, Americans sense a kind of freedom to explore, to move among the various booths and watch the jesters and jugglers, magicians and shamans, pastors and priests.[16] Bright colors attract their attention. Here they dabble in Goddess spirituality. There they discuss the earth as Gaia. In one corner they are encouraged to think positively about themselves, in another to discover wholistic approaches to health. Some take up yoga; others find meaning in Native American sweat lodge rituals. Some channel. Others meditate. The booths are endless.

Meanwhile, traditionalist and progressivist Christians who remain in the ruins of the old cathedral are huddled on both sides of a dividing wall. They are trying to decide how best to proceed in light of the destruction of the old cathedral. They watch as Americans gaily play at the county fair, drawn to this booth and that booth, having the time of their lives. They stand in the cathedral ruins and holler at the people enjoying the fair, "Hey, you're supposed to find God over here, not over there!" No one pays much attention. There's nothing much in the ruins to attract their interest.

This context necessitates a new approach by the church. It must learn to watch instead of be watched. It must engage in dialogue instead of evangelistic manipulation. And it must learn to ask questions instead of constantly spouting off answers. Christians who are concerned about the church's ineffectiveness might ask fairgoers about their individual spiritual interests:

- "What do New Agers believe?"
- "Why do you practice yoga?"
- "I find it interesting that you believe in reincarnation. What makes it so believable to you?"

By asking such questions, Christians exhibit humility, a trait the church rarely expressed when its spiritual domination was unchallenged. Perhaps that is why fairgoers today have so much trouble accepting the essential truths of the Christian faith. We might compare the church to a television cable company that has no competition and, thus, doesn't worry much about customer satisfaction. Then suddenly, when a competitor moves in, many of its customers switch to the new service, and the church is left scratching its head, wondering what happened to the masses.

 The Bible itself provides the solution for overcoming the schism.

The church has always looked to the Bible when it needed a makeover. But even as it looks to the Bible, it must also look at itself. The Scriptures must become a kind of mirror by which the American church in the late twentieth century gauges how effectively it reflects God's vision for the church.

The Wall

I recently led a Bible study on the book of Ephesians at a little church in rural Georgia. Together we wrestled with God's vision for the church. We talked about the way in which Christ had torn down the dividing wall between Jew and Gentile. We discussed how God had placed the church at the center of God's plan for the entire cosmos.

The church's patriarch, a kind-looking, white-haired gentleman, suddenly spoke up.

"Something's bothering me," he said.

"What is it?" I asked, certain that I had probably said something with which he disagreed.

"Well," he responded. "I'm looking around at this group of church people here—and everybody looks just like me. We're all well off; got nice houses; live good, clean respectable lives. We're all white, and we all have the same doctrine. Now, you tell me, is that really who we're supposed to be?"

His point was well-taken! The modern church in the late twentieth century only rarely reflects the church God intended. This is no great revelation. The church always falls miserably short of God's expectations for it. But the reality that it will always fail should never become an excuse for not striving for perfection.

The church will soon find itself in a postmodern context in which it scarcely recognizes itself. It will live on the margins and not at the center of its culture. But though the coup against it will be painful, the church may discover that it is much easier to practice Christianity on the margins than it is to live it out from the power corridors of society.

This will not be the first time that the church has lived on the edge. Once upon a time, a group of Christians found themselves relegated to the margins of society. They were powerless people, persecuted and generally ignored by the wider culture. Few people believed the story they told—that Jesus, a Palestinian Jew, was actually God and that he had entered into human existence in order to identify with sinners and proclaim the coming kingdom of God.

This Jesus performed miracles of healing. He turned water into wine. He detested all forms of self-righteousness and loved tax collectors and prostitutes. He preached a message of radical inclusiveness. He warned that anyone who ignored the hungry, the poor, and the prisoners would also, in turn, be ignored by God. He called upon his followers to love their enemies, turn the other cheek when wronged, and follow behind him in a journey of self-denial.

Following Christ's death and resurrection, the Holy Spirit visited itself upon the church, bringing a new kind of empowerment and vitality. The grand Christian story was hindered by only one grave threat, a division between Jewish and Gentile Christians over the nature of the faith. Were Gentile Christians to follow the Jewish law? Or were all Christians to be free of such constraints?

The fissure seemed almost insurmountable. Then, almost as suddenly as it had reared its ugly head, it disappeared. It ended because it was no longer relevant. The diversity of the Roman empire and the tenacity of the enemies of the faith necessitated a united front. The Jewish/Gentile schism fell by the wayside in order that the faith itself might survive.

This story, contained in the biblical text itself, has much to say to the American church as it faces the twenty-first century. Internal divisions, even those as destructive as the Jewish/Gentile schism or the traditionalist/progressivist schism can be overcome. Indeed they must be overcome if the church is to survive at the margins of society.

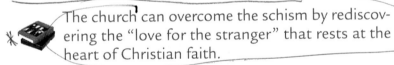

The church can overcome the schism by rediscovering the "love for the stranger" that rests at the heart of Christian faith.

As the world grows smaller, its diversity becomes increasingly apparent. American Christians now interact with strangers on a daily basis. I refer, of course, to people who are not like me—who dress differently from me, worship a different god from me, or speak another language. I refer also to strangers within my own church or denomination who think differently from me on the basic theological, ethical, and political issues of the day.

Strangers from India run the motel down on the interstate. Strangers from Japan build a huge metals plant out on the edge of town. Strangers of the Islamic faith wear their colorful robes and white hats around town. Strangers within my own church announce their affinity for a pro-choice position on abortion or for prayers in public school. They proclaim their opposition to capital punishment, their membership in the Christian

Coalition, or their support of People for the American Way. Their moral values are different from my own, and yet they worship the God of Jesus Christ. They are strangers within the Christian house. They live and move and breathe at a different end of the Christian spectrum. But they claim a place in the family of faith.

The church at the beginning of the twenty-first century finds itself in desperate need of a theology of "otherness." It must recover the "love of the stranger" that rests at the very heart of the church's identity. This love for "others" rarely exhibited itself in the modern American church. It didn't have to. Americans masked ethnic, theological, and socioeconomic differences by forming denominations based primarily upon such differences. "Others" established their own denominations. And, of course, other religions, if they existed at all, were relegated to the margins of society.

Churches in the South have been peculiarly influenced by this notion of "sameness." The American South has always been a culture unto itself. Southerners grew up with little religious diversity. And the only ethnic diversity was that which existed between the black and white races. In such a context, these churches barely had to deal with "otherness" at all.

Recently, Miroslav Volf, a Croatian and Pentecostal theologian, has called for the church to "place otherness at the center of theological reflection."[17] Volf's perspective emerges out of his own pain over "ethnic cleansing" in the Balkans. He hopes that a theology of otherness can assist Orthodox and Catholic Christians in that bitterly divided region to overcome some of their differences.

He draws attention to Elie Wiesel's description of the stranger as

> someone who suggests the unknown, the prohibited, the beyond; he seduces, he attracts, he wounds—and he leaves. . . . The stranger represents what you are not, what you cannot be, simply because you are not he. . . . The stranger is the other. He is not bound by your laws, by your memories; his language is not yours, nor his silence.[18]

In light of this definition, Volf insists that the church must reflect upon its own identity as "the stranger" if it is to respond to the strange world of the "other."

Ironically, the church itself was intended to live in the world as an "other." It was to swear allegiance to a kingdom that could not be seen. It was to reflect this kingdom in every way, but especially in its relationship to other human beings. Christians were to be in the world but not of the world.

Instead, Christians quickly identified with the world. Their socioeconomic differences reflected the economic realities of the world. Their racial differences reflected the racial differences of the wider culture. And recently, their theological differences have reflected the political differences of the world. Traditionalists stand on one side of the political spectrum, while progressivists usually stand on the other side. Political realities dictate theological perspectives!

The church has forgotten that citizenship in the kingdom of God results in the creation of a new people who cannot be divided by race, creed, or differing political agendas. Christians are to be people of a particular culture, whether that be American, Chinese, traditionalist, progressivist, Anglo-European, or African-American, who are able to lift themselves above their particular context to embrace the stranger. As Volf points out, "Christians are not simply aliens to their own culture; they are aliens that are at home in every culture, because they are open to every culture."[19]

This does not mean that Christians must accept the beliefs of other religions any more than it means that they must adopt the political agenda of a particular political party. But it does mean that Christians are to embrace people of other religious, theological, and political persuasions. Their purpose for existence is to overcome difference, not to create it. They, of all people, are to be most aware of the cultural realities that divide human beings. They are to value what is good in their own cultural context. But, at the same time, they are to lift themselves above their particular context in order to point to a universal kingdom in which religious, theological, and cultural differences will no longer exist.

My father first modeled for me this theological idea of the embrace of the stranger in his role as a Southern Baptist missionary in the Philippines and later in Singapore. He once participated in a Hindu funeral, offering prayers for the family and assisting in the building of the funeral pyre. He carefully nurtured relationships with Catholics and Muslims that were based upon mutual respect and admiration. Though unabashedly Christian, he never seemed to enter a relationship with another human being with the explicit purpose of making a Christian of him or her. Rather, he entered the relationship with the simple goal of becoming friends and breaking down walls. His greatest legacy to me is this embrace of strangers.

The sin of exclusion has destroyed this essential Christian idea. I do not harbor any illusions that traditionalist and progressivist Christians will embrace each other simply because I point out that exclusion of the stranger is sinful. But a Christian who cannot embrace the stranger who sits across the aisle in the sanctuary or who votes a different political agenda at the annual convention will never be able to embrace a stranger who doesn't sit in the church at all.

Jesus had a way of turning the tables on religious people. He called into question the whole notion of exclusion that rested at the heart of first-century Judaism. He feasted with tax collectors and prostitutes. He included the excluded, namely women, lepers, and the demon-possessed, despite the fact that these people were the unclean people of Jesus' day. This inclusion flew in the face of Jesus' opponents. He made his point: "The real sinner is not the outcast, but the one who casts the other out."[20]

What does this mean for the great divide that exists between traditionalist and progressivist Christians? Can the politics of exclusion give way to the embrace of the stranger? I very much hope that it can. Volf points out that "forgiveness is the boundary between exclusion and embrace."[21] We certainly do not have to forgive each other. We can continue to promote our own agendas. We can insist that we are right and that our enemies are wrong. The finger pointing can go on forever.

But other strangers watch. They observe from outside the Christian faith the behavior of those who are in it. They witness the damaging effects of the politics of exclusion. In a postmodern world, the strangers are everywhere. They inhabit our television screens, our convenience stores, our car washes, and our restaurants. They reflect upon these strange animals called Christians. And they wonder about this truth they proclaim.

It is time for the church to take seriously its obligation to reflect the unity of Christ's coming kingdom. It must remember that the real sinner is not the outcast but rather the one who casts the other out. True unity requires that we embrace each other by opening ourselves up in order that others might be taken in. This is the way of Christ. Traditionalist and progressivist Christians alike really have little choice in the matter. If we would embrace a world of strangers, we must first embrace the strangers who sit closest to us in the family of faith, the traditionalists or the progressivists whose theological ideas have most offended us.

The cultural war within Christianity has already ended. Neither side knows it yet, and neither side can claim victory. Oh, one side or the other won a small battle here or there. And a few skirmishes are still being fought. But, in the end, both groups will walk away empty-handed.

Traditionalists will walk away without the Christian America they so desperately sought. They will never turn back the clock to some "golden Christian" era of the past, even if they succeed in gaining political control of city councils and school boards. One can only hope and pray that their misguided effort to turn the Bible into a dry, dusty history or science book will also come to naught; otherwise, the damage will be irreversible.

Progressivists share the blame. They ripped the heart out of faith. Many of them insisted that miracles and healings and the Virgin Birth couldn't happen. Some even questioned the resurrection itself. They tap-danced around the tough questions, winked at parts of the Story, and came up with fancy words to explain it away. They also insisted that the Bible square with science. Their sin was equally damaging to the church. When it came to a choice between science or faith, they chose science. They insisted that scientific truth was the highest form of truth. And they waged a campaign to convince the faithful that you could rip the super-natural heart out of the thing and still have something left to die for.

Neither group could just let the faith be. They couldn't let the stories stand. They had to make them fit. They had to wedge the Christian story into a little science box. Traditionalists reduced it to the lowest form of truth, the kind that answers "how" and "when" questions, when all the time God meant for it to answer the "why" question. And progressivists reduced the grand story of God to little more than a nice story to live by. The price we have paid for these half-truths is clearly evident in almost any American church on a Sunday morning. This brings me to the final reality the church must face in the twenty-first century.

> The only way the church can overcome this division is to submit itself to the truth of the Christian story no matter what differences exist between that story and other stories, including the scientific story.

Is there a way by which traditionalists and progressivists can come together to communicate the truth of God's grace and love to a postmodern world? Yes, there certainly is. Progressivists and traditionalists alike can recover the "foolishness of the cross." They can once again affirm the wonderful truth that nothing God has done makes any sense whatsoever. And yet God has still done it. The creation of the universe is nonsensical. We cannot explain it. We can certainly never describe God's reasons for doing it. God's choice of Israel out of all the nations of the world certainly makes little sense. Egypt or Assyria would have been a better choice. Yet God chose Israel.

We've spent centuries trying to explain the reasons behind Christ's death on the cross. When we're perfectly honest, none of our high and lofty explanations make any sense whatsoever. Some Christians have framed elaborate defenses of the resurrection. Other Christians have explained the resurrection away by insisting that belief in it is not an essential faith requirement. None of our explanations have fully satisfied anyone.

So, in the end, we're left with nonsense. Not a single doctrine or story or belief makes any sense. We will never prove any of it. The only place to start is with the foolishness of it all. I believe it. You believe it. Other people believe it. We believe that God became flesh and dwelt among us. And the power of it rests in that belief. It does not rest in any justification that I can make of it. It simply is. And no scientific proof can ever make it more believable to me than that.

This, then, is the middle way for a church torn apart by the culture war between traditionalists and progressivists. Let's recover our faith, the belief that what the Bible says is true. And that truth has nothing whatsoever to do with the proof science offers. It has everything to do with the truth I know in my heart. This grand biblical story is the story out of which I will live my life. This is what we offer to a world that desperately needs to know the truth of God's grace and love.

Conclusion

I once taught oral English at a university in the People's Republic of China. One day a Chinese student asked me a question.

"Dr. Nash," he said, "You have now experienced life under both a capitalist system and a communist system. You are very qualified to tell us which system is best. Which one do you prefer?"

I framed my response very carefully, for I did not want to offend my listener.

"Well," I said, "I think that both communism and capitalism have strengths and weaknesses. Under capitalism, a person has freedom to succeed in business or to fail. But should one fail, there is no safety net under that individual to assist him. Under communism, such a safety net exists. But individual initiative often suffers because of the lack of competition."

Dissatisfied with my answer, he asked again, "But which one is better?"

"Neither is better," I said. "The problem does not rest in the system, but rather with the people who run the system. Always it is the human desire for power that leads to the abuse of other people."

And so it is with the church. It is not fundamentalism or liberalism that is really the problem. God does not choose sides. God stands in both camps. And God stands outside both camps. The reality is that neither side is completely wrong nor completely right. The problem is not fundamentalism, conservative Christianity, moderate Christianity, or liberal Christianity. The problem is the finite perspectives through which all human beings view reality. And the only way to overcome the division is to recognize our finitude and chart a middle course that is wide enough for all God's people. This middle way begins with spiritual and communal renewal in the body of Christ, something both traditionalist and progressivist Christians desperately need. It is to that renewal that we now turn our attention.

The Wall

Notes

[1]James Davison Hunter, *Culture Wars: The Struggle to Define America* (New York: BasicBooks, 1991) 44-45.

[2]John H. Simpson, as quoted in Jeffrey Hadden and Anson Shupe, *Televangelism: Power and Politics on God's Frontier* (New York: Henry Holt & Co., 1988) 28.

[3]David Spangler, "The New Age: The Movement Toward the Divine," in *New Age Spirituality: An Assessment*, ed. Duncan S. Ferguson (Louisville KY: Westminster/John Knox Press, 1993) 80.

[4]See Robert Wuthnow, *The Restructuring of American Religion* (Princeton NJ: Princeton University Press, 1988) 100-131.

[5]The phrase "holy war" was first applied to the Southern Baptist controversy in 1984, when Roy Lee Honeycutt, president of the Southern Baptist Theological Seminary, speaking in a seminary chapel, declared war on fundamentalist leaders within the denomination.

[6]See Bill J. Leonard, *God's Last and Only Hope: The Fragmentation of the Southern Baptist Convention* (Grand Rapids: Eerdmans, 1990) and David T. Morgan, *The New Crusades: The New Holy Land: Conflict in the Southern Baptist Convention, 1969–1991* (Tuscaloosa AL: University of Alabama Press, 1996).

[7]Mark Wingfield, "Typical SBC Church Appears Growing but Is Declining," *Western Recorder*, 21 January 1997, 2.

[8]John Rolfe, "A Relation of the State of Virginia" (1616) in *The Virginia Historical Register and Literary Advertiser*, I (1848) 111-12, quoted in Perry Miller, *Errand to the Wilderness* (Cambridge MA: Harvard University Press, 1956) 119.

[9]George Marsden, *Fundamentalism and American Culture: The Shaping of Twentieth-Century Evangelicalism: 1870–1925* (New York: Oxford University Press, 1980) 49.

[10]Will Herberg, *Protestant, Catholic, Jew* (Garden City NY: Doubleday Anchor, 1960) 257-58.

[11]Walter Truett Anderson, *Reality Isn't What It Used to Be: Theatrical Politics, Ready-to-Wear Religion, Global Myths, Primitive Chic, and Other Wonders of the Postmodern World* (San Francisco: HarperSanFrancisco, 1990) 10.

[12]Jean-Francois Lyotard, *The Postmodern Condition: A Report on Knowledge* (Minneapolis MN: University of Minnesota Press, 1984. Reprinted from 1979 edition) 5.

[13]See Stanley Hauerwas and William H. Willimon, *Resident Aliens: Life in the Christian Colony* (Nashville: Abingdon Press, 1989) for a theological assessment of this "new world."

[14]See Pamela Dickey Young, *Christian Faith in a Post-Christian World* (Minneapolis MN: Fortress Press, 1995) 2.

[15]Bill J. Leonard, "Religion in the South: Profiles for the Future," *Journal of the South Carolina Baptist Historical Society*, Vol. 20 (November 1994) 10.

[16]Spangler, 80.

[17]Miroslav Volf, "Exclusion and Embrace: Theological Reflections in the Wake of 'Ethnic Cleansing,' " in William A. Dyrness, ed. *Emerging Voices in Global Christianity* (Grand Rapids: Zondervan, 1994) 23.

[18]Elie Wiesel, *From the Kingdom of Memory: Reminiscences* (New York: Summit Books, 1990) 59f.

[19]Volf, 27.

[20]Ibid., 32.

[21]Ibid., 38.

Chapter 3

The Dance

We played a flute,
but you would not dance!
We sang a funeral song,
but you would not cry!
(Luke 7:32 CEV)

America is enjoying a spiritual revival! Such a revival should be good news for a church that has an obligation to enhance the spiritual lives of its congregants. Unfortunately, this turn of events is not exactly the kind of revival the church expected! Good Baptists and Methodists and Presbyterians who once spent Saturday night studying their Sunday School lessons now spend that same time lighting scented candles in their living rooms and reading *The Celestine Prophecy*, a New Age bestseller, while the Benedictine monks of Santo Domingo de Silos "chant" Latin prayers in the background.

What has happened to cause this shift into spiritual "high gear"? Is it our heightened anxiety over an approaching millennium? Is it our frustration over a rapidly-changing world that seems to have lost its moral center? Is it the introduction of Eastern religions into the nation? Is it a desperate search for meaning?

What has happened is that postmodernity has arrived, and the church now lives in it! People have grown tired of the modern world with its extreme confidence in the power of science and human reason. They want something more—something mystical and spiritual. They want something that gives meaning to life. They no longer are attracted to rational arguments for the existence of God. They have discovered Mother Earth, crystals, stargazing, speaking in tongues, the Goddess, spiritual rebirth, ancient Native American emergence mythologies, and sacred places. In short, they have rediscovered faith.

This awakening is something along the lines of other "Great Awakenings" in American Christianity, though this latest one is radically different at its core. In the Great Awakenings of the eighteenth and nineteenth centuries, the church retained considerable control of spiritual transition. The nation's cultural center, after all, was primarily Christian and Protestant, and all Awakenings occurred within those boundaries.

But this latest "Awakening" is occurring outside Christian and Protestant boundaries. The church finds itself not at the center of the Awakening, but at its edge, trying either to exploit the current spiritual climate or denounce it as a trivialization of true spirituality.

Aaron Spelling, who gave us such titillating fare as "Charlie's Angels," "Models, Inc.," "Melrose Place," and "Beverly Hills 90210," says: "It is a huge awakening! A huge awakening! And I think we are going to see more of it instead of less."[1] He tried to cash in on it! His short-lived syndicated series, "Heaven Help Us," described the exploits of two newlyweds who died in a plane crash only to become angels under the guidance of super-angel Ricardo Montalban.

Two spiritual challenges confront the church as it moves from the modern world into this new postmodern awakening. The first challenge offers good news of a sort to the church because it signals that a time of spiritual opportunity is at hand. The good news is that people are spiritually hungry. The modern world has left people in a state of spiritual emptiness in which they sense a vacuum in their lives. The spiritual challenge to the church is to communicate the Christian gospel in such a way that it can fill this void.

But the second challenge that confronts the church is certainly bad news! And the bad news outweighs the good news! The bad news is that the modern world has also left most American churches in a state of spiritual emptiness. Many traditional churches do not possess the spiritual vitality necessary to survive the journey from modernity into postmodernity.

I do not say this lightly. It is the cold, hard truth. The nation's churches have become, for the most part, modern institutions. For decades they have operated in a context that has encouraged them to be well-ordered, rational, and efficient. In an effort to appeal to the widest cultural audience, churches have elevated mind over heart, reason over faith, and activity over contemplation.

As a result, many churches are empty spiritual shells that claim to be spiritually vital, but that are, in truth, spiritually dead. They have lived for the last thirty years in a kind of denial, deluding themselves into believing that they were making a difference in the world. Instead, they have been slowly moving down the highway to irrelevance. They have compromised themselves by identifying too closely with their culture and by confusing the form of spirituality with its substance. Churches have had the life wrung out of them by the modern compromise with science and rationalism.

More bad news! Most churches continue to carry on business as usual in the face of such dramatic transformation. They continue to assume that the people to whom they preach and minister today have the same spiritual concerns and were raised in the same religious context as the people to whom the church ministered in the 1950s. But this is simply not true. Too often, the church is investing its time and energy in kinds of ministry and teaching and worship that no longer meet spiritual needs.[2]

Hans Christian Andersen's fairy tale entitled "The Emperor's New Clothes" is a fitting spiritual parable for traditional churches in America today.

Once upon a time a vain emperor ruled over his kingdom. He loved clothes and spent all of his money purchasing new outfits. He loved to ride around the kingdom showing off his latest purchases, basking in the "oohs" and "aahs" of his subjects. One day two swindlers from a distant city arrived at the palace. They informed the gatekeeper that they were weavers and that they could weave the most beautiful garments in the world. And not only was their cloth beautiful, but it also had a magical quality about it that rendered it invisible to all but the wisest people in the world.

The emperor was impressed. "Not only will I own a beautiful new outfit," he thought, "but I will also be able to test the wisdom of my counselors and pick the brightest people for my cabinet."

He gave the swindlers some gold and asked that they begin work immediately.

They wove for months, pretending to use the fine gold thread provided to them by the emperor, while actually hiding it in their knapsacks. Soon the emperor grew impatient. He wanted to see the new clothes, but he decided it the better part of wisdom to send his prime minister first to test the man's wisdom.

Of course, the prime minister didn't see a thing. But he knew better than to admit his stupidity. So he pretended to see the clothes. "Oh, they are so beautiful," he said. "The emperor must see them at once." And he ran to spread the good news and to encourage a visit from the emperor.

Soon the emperor made his way to the weaving room where the swindlers held up the new clothes for his inspection.

"What!" thought the emperor. "I must be stupid. I see nothing. Oh, how terrible for me!" But he commented on the shape of the clothes, the bright colors, and the texture anyway—just so no one would know of his stupidity. And he called all of his advisors into the room to solicit their opinions. All were amazed at the beauty of the clothes, though they really saw nothing.

Soon the clothes were finished. The emperor hurried into the room to be clothed in his new finery. He carefully pretended to put on the shirt, the pants, the coat, and the rest of the ensemble. The swindlers pronounced him fully dressed.

Off he set on a grand parade through the town. The townspeople acted as if they loved the colors of the clothes, though none of them really saw anything. They were just afraid to appear stupid by pointing out the obvious.

Then a young boy cried out, "The emperor has no clothes!"

The townspeople looked at one another and nodded in agreement.

"He doesn't have a thing on," they said.

The emperor shivered and carried himself more uprightly, determined to live with the charade rather than to accept the truth. And he returned to his bedchambers, followed by his two gentlemen train-carriers, who continued carrying the train that really wasn't there.[3]

The church has no clothes! There—it's about time someone said it! The church swindled itself! It convinced itself that the finest clothes were the clothes of the modern world. Modern clothes were, after all, the clothes that any self-respecting religion should wear. And it wore its modern clothes proudly. It was obvious that modern people would not tolerate any nonrational explanation for reality. And so the church followed along behind modernity like a dumb sheep being led to the slaughter.

Oh, no, you are saying to yourself right now! How can this be? The church had to wear such clothes. These clothes were the finest clothes available. Such clothes allowed the church to appeal to rational minds, to influence its society, and to build a great legacy! Look at the impact the church has had upon our nation's morality. Look at the difference it has made in the lives of people. How can you say that the church is spiritually naked?

It is spiritually naked because, for the most part, the churches of America reach no one but themselves. Most churches grow because members move from other churches. Most churches grow because sometimes they are able to retain the children of their members. Most churches grow because it is "proper" for a certain segment of the American population to belong to a church. It looks good!

Churches are spiritually naked because they are irrelevant to many people in the wider culture. Only about one-fourth of the American population strongly agrees that "the Christian churches in my area are relevant to the way I live today."[4] What a sad statistic! Churches should be grateful that people are capable of distinguishing between Christian faith and the church as an institution. While Americans see little value in institutional Christianity, at least half of all Americans agree that the Christian faith is relevant to the way they live today.[5]

It is time for spiritual renewal in the church. There is no other option. The traditional churches that dot the American landscape must face this cold, hard truth. Church is boring. Worship is a humdrum repetition of the same old rituals week in and week out. Most American churches have ceased to be places of true spiritual vitality.

What can be done? Perhaps a new definition of "spirituality" is a logical starting point. After all, most local churches have adopted a kind of institutionalized spirituality that is conditioned by their local, denominational, and cultural heritage much more than it is influenced by scripture, Christian tradition, and relationship to God.

The church often understands "spirituality" to be the performance of certain kinds of activities—specifically, morning devotions, worship attendance, or Bible studies. But spirituality is properly defined as the creation and cultivation of an intimate relationship with God. It is actually a state of being or a relationship that is based, not upon activity, but upon intimacy.

We might think of spirituality as a kind of dance with God. Our goal in the dance is to follow God's lead—to step in the same direction in which God is stepping. It is God, after all, who understands the spiritual needs of humanity. It is God's Spirit that can best direct the church toward a meaningful spiritual relationship with God for itself and for the world.

God is introducing dance steps that are shaped by a new kind of postmodern music. As these new steps are introduced, the church experiences much anxiety. It continues to dance to the old beat. It refuses to acknowledge the need for a renewed spirituality that is adequate for a postmodern world. It protests that the old spiritual forms are adequate. And gradually the church gets further and further out of step with God.

It is time to get back in step with God. How is this best accomplished? First, the church must admit its preference for old dance steps that no longer effectively meet the spiritual needs of humanity. This requires the acknowledgment and confession of spiritual emptiness. Second, the church must open itself to the new spiritual dance God requires of it in a postmodern world.

The Old Modern Dance

The church cannot step to the new postmodern spiritual dance with God until it first identifies the old dance steps that are no longer effective. Such a process is painful. But the church has experienced such self-criticism before and survived to tell about it! In 1518, Martin Luther posted his call for spiritual renewal on the chapel door at Wittenburg in Germany. His Ninety-Five Theses were a clear appraisal of the spiritual corruption of the medieval church that unleashed the forces of reform and revitalized the church. His was a call for a new dance in the midst of the spiritual emptiness of the old dance of the medieval church.

Cries for spiritual reform are being heard from every corner of American Christianity today. Something is wrong! People are beginning to notice that "the emperor has no clothes." Voices of pastors, teachers, and laypersons are warning that the church must acknowledge its spiritual emptiness and reform its structures.

I want to add my voice to theirs by identifying eight realities the church must face if it is to change its modern dance with God to a postmodern dance. I am certainly no Martin Luther. But I do love the church. And I hope that my "eight theses," in chorus with others, can serve as a stimulus to a renewed spiritual dance in the church.

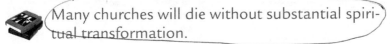 Many churches will die without substantial spiritual transformation.

I am referring, of course, to the institutional church, which is really the only church in this world that counts. We can protest that the church is more than a building—that it is, in fact, the community of Christians and not an institution at all. We can argue with the Calvinists that there is an invisible church that is the true church. We can assert that the universal church composed of all God's people on earth is more important than its separate little parts.

But, when all is said and done, such arguments are basically pointless. The most important church in the world is the local church at the center of town or down the street or out in the country that represents the God of Jesus Christ to its community. It is that church, composed of flesh and brick and wood and bone, that will beckon people to a living God or turn them off to God forever.

Thousands of these churches are about to die. That's right! The number-one religious story of the next century will be the deaths of thousands of local Christian churches. These churches will die slow and painful deaths brought on by changing demographics and their unwillingness to face the reality of their own spiritual inadequacy.

Many churches are already dead. A few members are hanging around to turn off the lights. But, for all practical purposes, the benediction is about to be pronounced. The church has become a hollow shell of its former self. The structures are still in place, but the heart has quit beating. Worship is empty, devoid of any real spiritual vitality. Business meetings are carried on more in the tenor of a community social club than a vital life-changing living organism. The doors stay open only to save face in the community or to assuage the guilt of those people whose ancestors founded the institution.

Mike Regele argues that a local church has only two options as its surrounding culture moves from modernity to postmodernity. It can die because of its resistance to change. Or it can die in order to be reborn as something new. Either way, the church as we know it will die.[6] Most churches are currently choosing the first alternative. The second choice is possible only if old structures and approaches and perspectives give way to new ones.

 Revivals, crusades, and other evangelistic services as they are now practiced in most churches are outdated relics of a dying modern world.

The spiritual structures that serve us well in one era often seem empty and meaningless in another era. Since about 1720, revivals, crusades, and other kinds of evangelistic services have been uniquely American forms of spiritual renewal. Revivals have served us well. They became a part of the rhythm of American church life, offering a seasonal opportunity for spiritual self-appraisal and the sharing of Christian faith beyond the church walls. But this form, as most churches now practice it, has served its purpose. It is spiritually empty. It no longer meets spiritual needs.

Revivals are fairly recent additions to Christian history, having emerged in about the eighteenth century in England and America as a backlash to the cold, hard scholasticism of Anglican religion. Revivals breathed life back into the church. People flocked to the anxious bench in the first and second Great Awakenings. They realized their deep need for repentance.

In the revivals, Americans rediscovered their own sinfulness and their need for God. They cried, they confessed, they hollered, they begged for forgiveness. They learned that salvation involved waiting—God visited salvation upon a person when God was ready. Revivals were messy affairs. Sins were confessed, often hysterically. Human beings were told to be ready. The Spirit moved without warning.

Today revivals are often well-ordered, carefully planned shells of their former selves. Church members attend out of loyalty to the institution. Revivals once were the primary entry point for non-Christians into the church. But few nonchurchgoers today will ever be drawn into a church because of a revival. Most revivals take one of two forms. Either they smack of pulpit-pounding, overzealous preachers who scare the devil out of people, or, and perhaps worse, they are carried on by churches that hold revivals because "it's the thing to do."

I recently attended a revival service. At first it seemed different from other revivals in which I had participated. We sang praise choruses. The evangelist wore a sports shirt and casual pants instead of a coat and tie. The church was packed on a Wednesday evening, which was no small feat in itself.

Then it quickly became all too familiar. The evangelist preached on the second coming of Jesus. He described hell in very vivid language, even warning the Christians in the bunch that they would be standing behind the throne of God, pointing the way to hell for those who had never professed faith in Christ. At the end of the sermon, he offered the invitation.

"Every head bowed and every eye closed," he said, exhibiting a total lack of originality. And he asked for a show of hands from the unsaved and the uncommitted. Then he warned them that if they did not confess Christ publicly, Christ would not acknowledge them before the throne of God. And he encouraged them to make their way "down the aisle."

And "down the aisle" they came, following in the grand cultural tradition of the American church on the frontier. It struck me that the only people who truly knew what to do in this situation were people who grew up in a revivalistic American subculture. I looked around at the homogeneity of the congregation, and my suspicions were confirmed. White, small-town southerners born and bred in a certain religio-cultural context were preaching a brand of Christianity that reached only other white, small-town southerners raised in the same cultural context. For all practical purposes, the church was preaching to itself. It was trapped in a certain understanding of spirituality that could be understood only by its own culture.

George Hunter argues that revivals and other traditional forms of outreach are incapable of reaching people outside the church:

> The harvest has changed from . . . corn to wheat. . . . We now enter wheat fields with our corn pickers. We fail to gather the harvest, and even destroy some of it while trying to gather it.[7]

That church was having a modern revival, not a postmodern revival. It had fallen behind the times. Its evangelical approach was effective only as a means to sustain itself, but it had little impact beyond its own walls.

 ## "Plans of salvation" are dead.

By "plans of salvation," I mean the canned approaches to sharing Christian faith that have been so much a part of the "technique" of the modern church.[8] I first used the "Four Spiritual Laws" tract in 1976 during a concert by my high school choir in a barrio in the Philippines. The sight of twenty freshly-scrubbed white faces drew quite a crowd to hear the music. After the concert, we were encouraged to make our way into the throngs of people to share "The Four Spiritual Laws."

I targeted one young man near the stage and slowly made my way over to him.

"Did you enjoy the concert?" I asked.

"Oh, very much," he responded. "You sing so beautifully!"

Without missing a beat, I moved on to the true purpose for my inquiry. "Have you ever heard of the 'Four Spiritual Laws?' " I asked.

"Certainly!" he said.

"You have?" I said incredulously. We had not been prepared for this eventuality!

"Oh, yes!" he said. "I belong to the Campus Crusade staff. You go find someone else to witness to!" And he pointed out into the crowd.

Mortified, I took refuge behind our choir's bus until the rest of the choir had completed the task! That experience began a lifelong antipathy for "canned" evangelism.

The very phrase "plan of salvation" smacks of a modern approach to sharing the Christian faith. It is neat, systematic, individualistic, well-ordered, and efficient. It is designed to spread the gospel to the greatest number of people in the shortest amount of time, which is certainly a modern goal if there ever was one! Plans of salvation such as the "Roman Road," the "Four Spiritual Laws," and other tract-like approaches to faith certainly served their purpose in modernity. Millions of people entered the Christian faith through just such a methodology. Methods worked in modernity. Faith was viewed as a process of quick, simple steps. In the modern world, people accepted the notion that, to be a Christian, all one had to do was to "pray the sinner's prayer."

I often tell my students that the history of Christianity in America has been a history of salvation occurring more efficiently and more quickly with the passage of time. This process squares nicely with the increasing efficiency that occurred in every other area of American life. Americans developed more efficient methods of production in factories. They developed more efficient methods of transportation and communication. And they developed more efficient methods for sharing the Christian faith.

Such approaches worked quite well in modernity when Christianity still dominated American culture and churches were viewed as Christian factories. The only spiritual option available to most Americans was the Christian church. The only way to be spiritual in America was the Christian way. So, the church produced Christians in much the same way that a modern factory produced goods. It pumped Christians out in a kind of assembly line. Once you had been stamped with a date, you were sent out in the world to start new factories and produce more Christians.

I am not attacking this approach to faith. It succeeded far beyond the wildest expectations of the church. Millions of people entered Christianity through the methodological door of a "plan of salvation." Such approaches still work well when persons can immediately move into a spiritually vital community of faith. But herein lies the problem. Most churches are no longer spiritually vital. And most people are no longer interested in being part of a church assembly line. Such plans have served their purpose.

 Being Christian in America must mean more than simply the avoidance of eternal punishment.

The problem that now confronts the church as it seeks to share the good news is that what worked in the efficient, pragmatic, rational modern world will not work in the postmodern world. Postmodernity is characterized by such adjectives as inefficient, nonrational, meaningful, open-ended. Postmoderns are seeking a relationship with God that is dynamic and life-changing.

As a result, postmodern people are interested in process, not event. "Becoming a Christian" for the postmodern church must mean something far different than it did in the modern world. For the modern church, it referred to the moment of salvation when one was "saved." The pragmatic event of salvation allowed the new Christian to avoid something (namely, the fires of hell) rather than to experience something (namely, a relationship with God).

Whether the church intended this interpretation or not, it nevertheless wormed its way into the popular mind-set and sapped the spiritual vitality of the church. People entered the Christian faith out of fear. To be in the door was enough. It got you what you needed. For every faithful Christian who viewed salvation as the beginning of a lifelong relationship to God, there were dozens who entered Christianity for a simple, static reason—to avoid the danger of eternal punishment.

And the church encouraged this fear. It was, after all, the quickest and easiest way to bring people into the kingdom of God. It worked quite well in a modern world in which people subscribed to a single Christian reality. Everyone believed in heaven, and everyone believed in hell. Being a pragmatic, modern institution, the church focused its time and energy on the approach that worked. But, by focusing most of its attention on the eternal destinations of its constituents, the church failed to give sufficient attention to enhancing the spiritual lives of its people.

Times have changed! People don't have to believe in heaven, hell, Jesus, or Satan. In fact, 60 percent of the American public now rejects the notion that Satan is a living being.[9] People can believe in reincarnation or a dawning new age. They can seek liberation from the cycle of suffering through Buddhism, or they can look forward to Nirvana. The Christian truth does not have to be accepted by them as the "Truth."

As long as the wider culture accepted the reality of hell, American churches could rest easy. People had to at least become Christian to avoid hell. So the church grew lazy. It could ignore the much harder task of enhancing the spiritual lives of people in this world. It didn't need to spend much time on prayer, meditation, or worship. These could be ignored. People came to church to secure their spiritual status in the next life and not necessarily to enhance it in this life.

The idea of hell gave the same power to the church in the modern world that the idea of purgatory gave to the church of the Middle Ages. In both instances the church abused its power by offering cheap grace to the faithful. In the medieval church this cheap grace was bought with money that assured that one could escape purgatory. In the modern world, such power has enabled the church to scare people into its walls without then providing an adequate spirituality to sustain them in daily life.

 Church members must stop "inviting people to church" and start inviting people to Christ.

An older woman in her sixties approached me shortly after I had pronounced the benediction on the Sunday evening worship service. She told me about her next door neighbors who regularly refused her invitation to attend church.

"What can I do to get them to church?" she asked.

I confessed that I knew of no simple response to her dilemma. Most churchgoers have enough trouble getting themselves and their families to church on a weekly basis without worrying about the neighbors.

"Why do you want these people to come to church?" I asked.

She looked at me like I was crazy!

"So they will become Christians," she thundered.

"Oh, that's different," I said. "You don't want to invite them to church then. You really need to invite them into the kind of relationship with Jesus Christ that you have. Hopefully, then, their relationship with Christ will lead them to the church."

Why do Christians insist on inviting people to church instead of to the Christian faith itself? Two reasons come to mind. First, many American Christians do not feel confident enough in their own spiritual relationship with Christ to share that relationship with other people. Their Christianity is an inherited faith and not a personally vital faith. They had little choice in the matter. Spirituality was carefully meted out to them in a well-defined system of worship, Bible study, youth retreats, and programs. Careful spiritual boundaries were prescribed for them. Daily Bible reading was acceptable and even encouraged. Spirituality was institutionalized!

Second, there is the idea that it is proper to talk about God at church but improper to talk about God elsewhere. Such is the legacy of modernity. Every institution has its function. The function of the church in a well-ordered modern society is to offer a "place" to be religious. Faith is rendered impotent. It is acceptable to talk about Jesus at church, but unacceptable, and even embarrassing, to talk about Jesus at school or work.

This is clearly evident in the church's preoccupation with a professional clergy that protects the essential doctrines of the faith. The clergy went to seminary and "studied up" on Christianity. The laity came to view these religious professionals as the appropriate experts on faith. The clergy checked to ensure that everyone was doing Christianity in the proper way. I am reminded of this professionalization whenever a parent comes to me with a child and asks me as the religious professional to make sure the child is truly Christian. Thus, thousands of Christian parents miss out on the joy of sharing Christ with their own children. If laypersons don't feel competent enough to share Christ with a son or daughter, how can they possibly feel competent to share Christ with a friend or neighbor?

 The church must quit shoring up propositional truths about God while ignoring the need for an experience with God.

"Do you believe the Bible?" the man thundered from the rear of the room.

I certainly didn't appreciate his attitude.

"Sir," I responded, "Why would I waste my time working as a deacon in my local church and helping students prepare for Christian ministry in a Baptist college if I didn't believe the Bible?"

"I just heard that you religion professors don't believe the Bible," he said. "And I wanted to know if it was true or not."

I reassured him!

But his question stayed with me. It occurred to me that no two Christians in the world believe exactly the same thing about the Bible.

Obviously the various Protestant denominations differ in their understandings of the Bible.

What he really meant was, "Do you subscribe to the same set of propositions about God that I do?" I am sure that he was thinking about such things as the Virgin Birth, the miracles of the Bible, Christ's divinity, and so forth. And I would agree with him that such propositions about God are very important, even essential. These are the doctrines of the church that have been hammered out over the course of Christian history and that serve as a foundation for Christian thought and practice. But, in the modern world, the church has become spiritually unhealthy because of its overattention to doctrine and its inattention to Christian spirituality.

Christianity is now enslaved to this insistence on objective, propositional faith. But we hardly notice this enslavement because the scales have been unbalanced for so long. Too many sermons are devoted to the teaching of theological truth. And too few sermons assist faithful churchgoers to a deeper spiritual relationship with Jesus Christ. Pastors are too busy preaching the truth of an inerrant Bible or the Virgin Birth or the bodily resurrection to notice that church members have no spiritual relationship with God and little avenue for developing such a relationship in most local churches.

Such attention to doctrinal detail comes at a time when churches are desperately trying to attract a new adult generation of twenty- and thirty-somethings known as Generation X. Born between 1963 and 1977, Generation X-ers grew up in a postmodern world and tend to be suspect of religious dogma. Also known as baby busters, these young adults are drawn to churches in which worship is caring and relational and in which the truth of the Bible rests not in propositional assertions about God but rather in its application to the struggles of daily life.[10]

Generation X is issuing a prophetic warning to the church. And it is a warning that must be heard! Intellectual assent to the basic tenets of faith is only one part of the journey toward God. Emotional and relational aspects to that journey are of equal importance and must receive their just due in the worship and community life of the church. Other religions and spiritualities stand ready to meet these needs if the church should fail to do so.

American Christians have, for much too long, claimed divine sanction for their nation and for their religious institutions.

I sometimes play a little game with my college students by offering a quarter to the person who comes closest to identifying the year in which the following statement was made:

> The people of the United States come nearer to a parallel with Ancient Israel than any other nation upon the globe.[11]

The exercise helps students to identify the pervasiveness of the mythology of divine chosenness that rests at the heart of American Christianity. The statement could have been made in 1997 or in 1777. It was actually spoken in 1799. One thing is certain: For 220 years, American Christians have been quite confident of their own divine election.

Such confidence has been both blessing and curse. It has provided the foundation for a vast American missionary force that has extended the Christian faith around the world.[12] But it has also resulted in the idolization of the American nation and an uncritical allegiance to the institutional structures of American Christianity.

The American church is trapped by this idolization of cultural and institutional forms. The American flag inappropriately graces the sanctuaries of many American churches, mocking the notion that the church of Jesus Christ has no political or geographical boundaries. Patriotic songs and the pledge of allegiance to the American flag dominate the worship service on a Fourth of July Sunday. American children repeat the pledge of allegiance during Vacation Bible School each summer.

I watched during the Persian Gulf War as Christians wrestled with the dilemma of praying for the nation's soldiers. An "us vs. them" mentality seemed to prevail. Flags hung from the fronts of Christian churches. Ministers prayed for "our" troops. I heard few prayers for scared Iraqi soldiers and their families. I wondered how many American Christians even noticed how quickly the church championed its culture and lined up behind the nation as a kind of societal cheerleader.

But it is not only the nation that co-opts the spiritual energy of the church. All too often, churches are enslaved to denominational and institutional structures that inhibit or destroy spiritual vitality. In my own days as a pastor I was amazed by the number of institutional and denominational Sundays that occupied the church year. Churches observed College Day, Senior Adult Sunday, Men's Day, July Fourth Sunday, Thanksgiving Sunday, Sunday School Promotion Sunday, and Race Relations Sunday. Leander Keck points out that in all such services the focus of worship is turned away from God and toward something else.[13] Churches become bound to certain institutionalized forms of spiritual growth that are usually produced by a denominational publication board.

As a result of such institutional and denominational enslavement, churches took little responsibility for their own spiritual vitality. To be a spiritually vital church was to follow the program laid out by the larger denomination. Church members were plugged in and turned on to a particular denominational program of spiritual growth. Churches rarely had to develop their own spiritual avenues from within the congregation itself. Now that denominational structures are diminishing in importance, churches find themselves without an adequate spirituality that can support the life of the congregation.

 The church refuses to admit its guilt in failing to provide for the spiritual needs of people.

If I've heard it once, I've heard it a thousand times in a thousand different forms!

- "People receive from worship exactly what they put into worship."
- "We're not here to entertain people; we're here to help them worship."
- "We're not going to sing praise choruses in our worship service. Our service is going to have some dignity to it."
- "These young people today just aren't committed to the church."
- "We're going to have Sunday night church no matter what."

The message in all of these statements is very much the same. The church has performed its worship and ministry obligations in a particular way for many years. What has worked for past generations should work for present and future generations! If people are not experiencing spiritual growth and vitality, then it must be their own fault. The blame for spiritual emptiness is subtlely shifted away from the church and toward "those who aren't as committed as we are."

Rare is the church that pauses to look honestly at its own spiritual strengths and weaknesses. Churches tend to be places of spiritual self-congratulations where past accomplishments are celebrated, but little attention is paid to the current spiritual climate. A church is a religious institution, and religious institutions are notoriously bad at assessing their weaknesses. But no church can effectively prepare itself for ministry in a postmodern and twenty-first-century world until it confesses that it is not yet prepared for such ministry. It must come to a point that it can admit that its modern clothing is not adequate for a postmodern world.

It must confess its shortcomings. If a church has been content to minister only to itself, then it must confess that contentment before it can move on to ministry outside its own walls. If it has been content with week-long revival services that rarely bring people to faith in Christ, then it must confess its enslavement to old forms and then search out something that is more spiritually vital. If Sunday night worship consists of a couple of hymns and a halfhearted sermon before a bored handful of church members, then the church ought to seek God's forgiveness for making a mockery of worship. It should then kill such a service before it kills the church.

Spiritual rebirth cannot occur until old spiritual forms that have lost their vigor have been buried deep in the earth. I would suggest that a local church begin this process of spiritual transformation by asking its membership to assess its spirituality. Ask the following questions:

- Does the church meet your spiritual needs? Why or why not?
- How spiritually meaningful are the worship services and Wednesday evening prayer service?
- What is the most spiritually meaningful event you have experienced in the past year? Why was it meaningful?
- How can the church cultivate more meaningful spiritual experiences for you in the coming year?
- What do you believe to be your own spiritual inadequacies? How can the church help?

Such introspection allows for a spiritual evaluation of the congregation. It assesses the strengths and weaknesses of worship, prayer, and other spiritual forms that are essential to a spiritually healthy congregation. But such assessment is only the first step. Now the church must begin to assess its worship services and other structures to begin to recapture spiritual vitality. It must open itself to the tugging of the Spirit in a new day!

The New Postmodern Dance

With the coming of postmodernity, a new spiritual reality has dawned. We live in an age of easy belief. Churches are surrounded by a culture that is radically pluralistic, highly spiritual, antidogmatic, and nonrational. In such a climate, there must be a rebirth of Christian spirituality. A new kind of Christianity must emerge that is exciting, unapologetic, confident, resourceful, and courageous. It must be a Christianity that is freed from the modern approach to the faith that has dominated in the American church.

Loren Mead believes that the American church must face three startling new realities in the late twentieth century:

• We can no longer assume that everyone in the United States is a Christian.
• The local community and the local church are no longer synonomous with each other.
• The front door of the church is once again a doorway to missions much as it was in the early church.[14]

I want to propose a whole new paradigm for Christian spirituality that takes seriously this new world that now surrounds the church. This new spiritual dance is unique in that it draws from the full range of Christian experience. It is not a Baptist dance or a Catholic dance. It does not derive from a conservative theology or a liberal theology. Such lines no longer apply. Now Christianity must present a united front to the world. And that united front must include a spiritual dance that is uniquely Christian, highly missionary, deeply devotional, and, above all else, intensely meaningful.

The revitalization of Christian spirituality in a postmodern world is contingent upon eight new dance steps that must be taken in one form or another within local churches. As members become proactive in initiating these actions, a renewed spirituality will take hold within the congregation. As one partner begins to dance with God in a new way, other partners will follow. Here are the eight new steps.

 Embrace the Scriptures.

We have "believed" the Bible. For almost a century now, Christians have feared a loss of confidence in the Scriptures. The church has waged a mighty battle to protect the Bible. We have insisted upon its absolute truth and that such truth is theologically, scientifically, historically, and geographically verifiable. It must be believed.

But our very insistence upon the believability of the Bible is the first step toward rendering the Bible impotent. Among all the holy books of the world's religions, the Bible stands alone as the book that seems most threatened by serious scholarly challenge to its authenticity. My conversations with Muslims, Hindus, and Buddhists lead me to conclude that these persons do not feel similarly threatened by scholarly assessment of the Koran or the Bhagavad-Gita or the Dhammapada.

Why not? Perhaps it is because faithful Muslims and Hindus and Buddhists consider such challenges to be insignificant. Their holy books serve as the sources for stories that shape their lives. Scholars can dissect away; it really doesn't matter. The stories of these faiths still hold true for those who believe them. Questions about the scientific verifiability of these books cause hardly a ripple among the faithful.

Christians must embrace the Bible in this same way if a renewed spirituality is to take hold in the church. We can no longer allow our notions about the truth of the Bible to be dictated by the scientific method. We must recognize that, in a postmodern world, science is not the sole arbiter of truth, nor is its kind of truth necessarily the highest form of truth. The truth of the Bible rests not in its scientific verifiability, but rather in its story and in the people whose lives are transformed by this story.

In the modern world, propositional faith served as the foundation for the stories of the faith.[15] We knew what we believed, and we made the stories of faith conform to that body of truth. In the process we allowed the truth of the Bible to be subsumed under the truth of science. God's mystery and transcendent power over human life and the creation became something that could be explained by science. Faith became contingent upon "believing the Bible" and not upon participation in the grand story of God's relationship to humanity.

In a postmodern culture, the stories of the faith must serve as the starting point in the search for truth. We now live in an imaginative and story-conscious world in which one's faith perspective is dictated by life-transforming stories. Christianity must cultivate once again the ability to tell the life-changing stories of the faith and then to assist persons to live life out of those stories.

Leander Keck says that "the time is at hand to stop worrying about the Bible and to start worrying about ourselves."[16] His affirmation provides a hinge for the transformation of our understanding of the Bible. How do the sacred stories of faith transform my life? This is the question Christians must learn to ask themselves. The Bible must become a source of life-changing stories that all emerge from a single great story and that individually assist human beings in living inside the Story.

The focus in a postmodern world must be upon participating in the story that rests at the heart of the Bible. In the modern world, the stories of David and Goliath, of the Creation, of Paul's shipwrecks, of Jesus and the woman with the hemorrhage, led us to ask, "How can I defend these stories against those who don't believe them?" The burden of proof rested on the church's shoulders. Today we should ask a different question. "How should I live in light of these stories?" The stories then become the shaping influences upon our lives, and the evidence of their truth resides not in scientific proof, but rather in the fact that Christians pattern their lives by them.

 Practice joyful worship.

Worship occurs when God's people gather to retell the Story, to realign their lives within the Story, and to praise God for the Story. Too many worship services in the modern world were directed toward propping up the Story rather than retelling it. Worship became an exercise in convincing dubious congregants that God truly existed or that the resurrection actually occurred. Great intellectual energy was expended to prove that a fish swallowed Jonah, that a virgin gave birth to the son of God, and that God created the world in six days. Such an approach made sense. After all, modern people loved to doubt, so doubt became the demon to be exorcised through worship.[17]

In the process, worship became joyless. Churches were so busy proving God that they failed to retell the Story in such a way that people could find joy in it. Worship was somber and dignified. The focus was upon order and decorum and the intellectual defense of the faith. Doctrines of the faith were elevated at the expense of the full experience of the faith. The significance of a sermon was determined by its intellectual content or its apologetical brilliance. Sermons consisted of three points, carefully cultivated and sensible. After all, a well-ordered worship service ensured that the Christian faith would remain respectable to the outside world. Emotion was held in check. Each aspect of worship was carefully structured and controlled.

But postmodern worship must be something altogether different. It must celebrate the joy of life in Christ. It must be centered in the retelling of the Story in such a way that the worshipers find themselves inside the Story even as they worship. Modern worshipers sat on the outside looking into the Story. They analyzed the story—its characters, its plot, its plausibility. Postmodern worshipers want to sit inside the Story itself. They want to embrace it and live it.

I recently participated in two worship services during Advent that illustrate the difference between modern and postmodern worship. On one December Sunday morning, I preached from the story of John the Baptist in Luke 3. The theme of the service was repentance. The service was modern in every way. Hymns were sung. Prayers were prayed. The congregation listened to the essentials of the story. In order to be ready for Christmas, I said, we must engage in confession and repentance of sins.

After church, the faithful departed with the usual "Good sermon, preacher" comments at the front steps. I left church mildly dissatisfied. The Story had suffered in the telling. John the Baptist had called us to repentance, but we had stood afar off. The congregants had not gathered close enough to the Jordan River to get their feet wet.

I wrestled through the following week with the text for the next Sunday, this time Luke 1, the Magnificat, with its themes of liberation. My concern was to involve the congregation in the text itself, to bring the faithful into the Story, and then to help them find themselves in it. The choir sang about Mary's thoughts when confronted by the angel.

Then I stood to preach. The pianist softly played the music to Andraé Crouch's "Soon and Very Soon" as I read the Scripture. Then the congregation stood to sing it with me.

> Soon and very soon,
> We are going to see the King;
> Soon and very soon,
> We are going to see the King;
> Soon and very soon,
> We are going to see the King.
> Hallelujah! Hallelujah!
> We're going to see the King.
>
> No more crying there,
> We are going to see the King;
> No more crying there,
> We are going to see the King;
> No more crying there,
> We are going to see the King.
> Hallelujah! Hallelujah!
> We're going to see the King.[18]

I talked of the songs of faith and the themes of Mary's song, of the lowly being lifted up and the mighty humbled. I ended with these words from the great Charles Wesley hymn, "O, For a Thousand Tongues to Sing."

> Here Him, ye deaf;
> his praise, ye dumb,
> Your loosened tongues employ;
> Ye blind, behold your savior come;
> And leap, ye lame, for joy.[19]

We stood to sing these words and its companion verses as the hymn of response. Then the pianist segued into "Soon and Very Soon." A soprano took up a descant. The words thundered from the congregation, powered by Mary's song—"God All-Powerful has done great things for me, and his name is holy" (Luke 1:49, CEV). Mary's words became our words. Mary's story became our story. This time, I could hear the congregants singing as they left church. No one said a word about the sermon. "We really worshiped today," a man observed. I left singing, too.

 Live out the faith.

This new dance step takes seriously the truth that the postmodern world is a place of easy belief. Postmodern people desperately want a sense of meaning and purpose in life. This is good news for the church. Danny Stiver insists that "removing the confining strictures . . . of reason has created a greater opportunity for a reasoned dialogue between faith and the world, not less."[20] This search for meaning will create an environment of open inquiry into the basic questions of human existence. And Christianity will be freed from the modern impulse to prove itself to a doubting humanity.

In such a context, the Christian faith can be communicated easily and naturally. Christian people have an advantage in such an environment. Many of us have lived in the light of God's story of Jesus Christ for years without the need for scientific verification of that life or the death and resurrection that make it so powerful. The meaningful life I live as a result of this story can speak volumes to others who now desperately seek a story by which to ground their own lives.

But shouldn't we still be concerned to prove that the story of Jesus is the only story by which life should be lived? No, at least not initially. The burden of proof rests not in the words we say, but rather in the lives of those of us who live according to the Story. The modern world provided incontrovertible proof that no amount of prooftexting or reasonable dialogue could prove Christianity to be the only true faith. Only the joyful lives of Christian people who live in the light of that Story can make Christianity believable.

So let's quit insisting, at least at the beginning of our dialogue with nonbelievers, that our story is the only story. This old modern dance step is no longer effective. Instead, let's admit that our story is based upon our view of reality, and that, yes, there are many stories out there that people are free to believe. This does not mean that we compromise the gospel story in any way. It still is the single true Story. We believe it, and we encourage others to see it. We live life by this story and share it freely and joyfully with others. It is our story, and we quite naturally would want others to experience the abundant life we live as a result of its shaping influence.

Karl Barth once compared the biblical story to the experience of looking out a window and seeing a crowd of people pointing to something above the house that cannot be seen by us. We know by their expressions that what they see is intensely pleasurable. Their happiness is evident in the smiles on their faces. Something good is happening, and they keep beckoning us outside to see what they see.[21] Our interest is piqued by the obvious joy that infects their faces and their lives. We are drawn as much by their inward excitement as by their outward actions.

The Christian faith must be communicated in just such a way if it is to be communicated at all in a postmodern world. The objective insistence upon the truth of the Christian faith must take a secondary place behind the joyful living out of that faith. Christianity is now competing with other faiths that also promise spiritual meaning and a grand story by which to live one's life. It cannot compete on the level of the objective truth of its story, for such truth will never be proven. But it can compete when the lives of its followers offer obvious proof of its spiritual vitality.

 Take risks.

Risk taking has always been an intrinsic element of the life of faith. A religion that bids its followers to forsake mother and father, love enemies, and stand against oppression is a religion of risk. There is no such thing as life without risk in the kingdom of God. A church that fails to risk fails at the single most essential task of the church.

Now is the time for the church to take risks. It really has no choice. Everything about the way we have done church in American culture is up for grabs. Denominations are in decline. Clergy and laity alike are confused about what ought to be done to enhance the spirituality of the congregation. Consultants stand ready to offer a hundred different solutions to a thousand different problems. But no one is more equipped to assist a local church than its own leadership.

Take a risk. This is perhaps the most difficult dance step of all. When a church leader, be it a clergyperson or a layperson, steps out on a risk, the other dance partners become anxious. They are forced to respond to the new pattern. They become antagonistic. They may even try to sabotage the dance. New dance steps are being introduced. And new steps are not easily learned.

Take small risks at first. Throw a monkey wrench into the fray, and then run out the door. As a church leader, begin with your committee members, the deacon body, or your Sunday School class. Announce that you would like to do things a little differently. Dump the old Sunday School quarterly for a couple of weeks and spend some time in prayer. Encourage your worship committee to attend worship services at other churches. Inform the ushers that the offering will be collected differently on a particular Sunday. Target at least one activity a week in the church and do it differently than it has ever been done before.

It is difficult in such an environment to introduce risk taking as an acceptable philosophy by which a church can undertake its various ministries. But it is essential. Help your congregation to understand that it is better to fail at a new ministry or worship idea than it is to remain mired in the same bog week after week. Engage in creative experimentation that is grounded in thoughtful planning, reflection, and prayer.

 Draw from other Christian traditions and the full resources of Christian history.

I regularly take my students to visit St. Bernard's Monastery and Retreat Center in Cullman, Alabama. The visit is always an intensely spiritual experience for the students as well as for me. We sit in the choir loft with the monks. The high ceiling of the church rises up above us and beckons our hearts and minds toward God. As the monks chant the Psalms, I find myself wondering why the prayers of the psalmist seem so much more intensely beautiful and meaningful in that setting than in any other context. I go home with a renewed spirit, empowered by the very words of the Bible as they were repeated by the Catholic monks of St. Bernard's.

The church only cheats itself when it fails to draw from the rich treasury of the full Christian tradition. We do not have to become Catholic or Baptist or Episcopalian or Methodist in order to appreciate the rich contributions these traditions can offer to any church that is seeking to recover or enhance its own spiritual vitality.

Many evangelical churches are terrible at the proper observance of Holy Week between Palm Sunday and Easter Sunday. We should allow Christians from other traditions to become our teachers for this vital week in the Christian year. Traditionally, we celebrate Palm Sunday and Jesus' triumphant entry into Jerusalem and then race as quickly as possible to Jesus' resurrection on Easter Sunday morning. In the meantime, we miss some of the most intensely spiritual moments in the life of the church and, thus, are not adequately prepared for the empty tomb.

We must learn from others the proper celebration of Maundy Thursday with its themes of spiritual preparation and humility through communion and foot washing. Yes . . . foot washing! It never occurs to us that we avoid washing feet for the very reason Jesus called upon his followers to practice it. It is a demeaning and humbling experience! Christians from other traditions can also teach us much about the proper and solemn celebration of Good Friday. It is on Good Friday, after all, that we confront our own participation in the death and crucifixion of Jesus Christ. On this day, Christians ought to put Jesus back on the cross, witness the cruelty done to him, and hear again his dying words.

We also must develop a knowledge of the full history of the Christian faith and the various approaches to Christian spirituality that have been an intrinsic part of that history. Several years ago, my wife asked a Sunday School class to spend a few moments in meditation as part of the lesson for the morning and in order to find some connection with God. Class members were taken aback. They protested that meditation was not a good practice for Christian people.

That class did not know that Christians have meditated for centuries! Meditation is not the sole province of such Eastern religions as Hinduism and Buddhism. It was practiced throughout Christian history by monks and mystics. And yet, thousands of Christians now flock to Eastern religions as a result of Christianity's failure to practice this vital spiritual form. A friend recently told me that she had become a Zen Baptist: "I still am a Christian," she said. "But I find in Buddhism the kind of quiet reflection that is absent in my church."

 "Celebrate" communion.

Communion offers a starting point for spiritual renewal in the church. The celebration of the Lord's Supper offers a doorway through which congregations can recover a sense of mysticism and contemplation in the life of faith. Unfortunately, the modern church has taken the Supper and wrung the life out of it with its emphasis upon cold, hard efficiency. Some churches act as if there is a script in the Bible that details the proper celebration of the Supper. This script must be followed to the letter. Only certain kinds of elements and serving pieces may be used. Only certain church leaders and/or the minister(s) can dispense the elements to the faithful, and this dispensing process can occur only on prescribed Sundays and according to a schematic drawing.

This attention to detail has turned the Lord's Supper into a mechanical and solemn affair that causes hardly a ripple in the spiritual lives of the faithful. Often it appears as a kind of afterthought to worship that is simply tagged on to the end of the service. Some churches fail to offer the Supper more than once or twice a year if at all.

And yet the Lord's Supper offers an essential spiritual moment in the life of a congregation. It ought to be the spiritual lifeblood of the church that reminds it of Christ's death and resurrection and that calls it to the "unity of the Spirit in the bond of peace." But several changes in its celebration are essential if a renewal of its observance is to occur.

It must be a celebration. The power of a communion service rests in the joy and fellowship that characterize it. Frederick Buechner says of the Lord's Supper:

> To eat this particular meal together is to meet at the level of our most basic humanness, which involves our need not just for food but for each other. I need you to help fill my emptiness just as you need me to help fill yours. As for the emptiness that's still left over, well, we're in it together, or it in us. Maybe it's most of what makes us human and makes us brothers.[22]

The Lord's table is always a place of celebration, for it is at the table that we find community and acceptance despite our brokeness and pain. It is at the table that we point ourselves toward a future Lord's table in a day when we will no longer be tempted to abandon God or each other. And, it is at the table that we draw strength from other people of faith whose lives, like ours, are in need of repair.

It must happen with more frequency. At least once a month, an entire service should be devoted to the celebration of the Supper. Hymns, music, and sermon in this monthly service should be directed toward the communication of one of the many spiritual truths that rests at the heart of the celebration: abandonment, humility, unity, love, betrayal, friendship, loyalty, liberation, oppression, sacrifice, and many more.

It should never happen the same way twice. The Lord's Supper provides a wonderful opportunity for creative worship services in which the worship theme determines the mode of celebration. If the theme is God's presence in time of suffering, then the congregation can be invited to the altar by pews to receive the bread and wine. If the theme of the service is the unity of the church as the body of Christ, then a large loaf of bread can be passed from pew to pew. If the theme is Christ's final abandonment, then the communion service can be carried on in absolute silence devoid of any words or music.

It must provide opportunity for a mystical encounter with God that leads to unity with God. Postmoderns are seeking mystical unity with God. Such mystical encounter is the stuff of the church, which has always insisted that an experience with God cannot be explained in a rational manner. It simply happens. And the church has a responsibility to provide occasions in which such experiences can happen.

 Reform the clergy.

Clergy in local churches will be the group whose roles change most dramatically in the cultural transition from modernity to postmodernity. Most seminary-trained ministers attended institutions that prepared them for ministry in a modern world. The educational emphasis was upon theology, apologetics, and practical ministry. Clergy were viewed as church leaders who set the general vision for the congregation and then assisted church members in attaining that vision. Ministry was carried out in a closed denominational system that provided the blueprint for spiritual growth and the boundaries for mission involvement.

Times have changed. The success of a minister's career is directly dependent upon that minister's ability to understand the new ministry context and re-envision his or her ministerial role. Churches have already experienced a transition from a trickle-down to a trickle-up approach to missions and ministry. I have witnessed this transition in my own church in recent months as church members have begun attending seminars with the ministers, searching out new kinds of programming, and engaging in local mission options.

In the modern church, such tasks belonged to the professional clergy. And, while many ministers welcome this refreshing new interest, some fear the loss of control over the church's direction. The new challenge for the clergy is to encourage such involvement while, at the same time, channeling spiritual energy in a direction that is beneficial to the whole congregation.

The new landscape of reality in American culture dictates that church leaders ask questions instead of provide answers. Ministers in the old, modern church were viewed as the professional "experts" who could provide answers to theological and practical questions. Ministers in a postmodern church will be viewed as participants in a common search for answers to such questions. The church can only be strengthened by such an approach as laypersons develop a sense of spiritual self-confidence and as ministers retreat into the background as cheerleaders in the process of spiritual enhancement.

In a postmodern church, ministers should view themselves as spiritual directors, who, because of their own close attention and allegiance to the way of Jesus, can enable others to find wholeness. The cultivation of a minister's own contemplative and devotional lifestyle has never been more important. But the modern notion that the contemplative lifestyle can be maintained solely through a "daily quiet time" coupled with the short reading of a devotional guide must give way to the postmodern idea of a wholistic spirituality that pervades all of life. Spirituality can no longer be viewed as a category in one's day that can be noted on a daily calendar. Every moment of the day is a spiritual moment, and the Christian minister must model this reality.

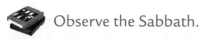 Observe the Sabbath.

The Sabbath can serve as a doorway to renewed spirituality in the life of a congregation. The observance of the Sabbath in an intentionally spiritual sense is largely ignored by most Christians today. And yet Sunday is already a welcomed interruption for most of us. It is a day of rest in which we worship, nap, read the paper, and take a short walk. A slight reorientation of the mind and heart can turn this day into a spiritual holiday that reminds us of the sacredness of time and space and reintroduces a sense of the holy into our lives.

I am certainly against the kind of Sabbath observance that was practiced earlier in this century when stores were closed and lawn mowing was banned. I do think, however, that the Sabbath can become a day that enhances our spiritual relationship to God. It can be a day in which we refuse to do anything that detracts from that relationship—such as balance the checkbook or buy groceries if such practices put us in foul moods. It can be a day in which we eat a Sabbath meal with our families and thank God for their presence in our lives. It can be a day when we take a walk around the neighborhood, look at the trees and sky and friends, and acknowledge the beauty of God's creation. And it can be a day when we take a nap without guilt and thank God for the gift of rest, that is an essential element of our lives.

The Sabbath affords us the opportunity to practice the kind of wholistic spirituality that is essential to the Christian life. On this single day, we can dance with God in an intentional way. And this day can become a model for the living out of other days as we heighten our awareness of our own spiritual dance with God. Most importantly, it provides us with the rare opportunity to reflect upon the distance between God and self and make the necessary changes that help to bridge the gap.

Conclusion

It is time for Christianity to seize the day. Never before in the history of the American nation has the population been so unquestioningly open to the mystery of Christ's life, death, and resurrection. Such a mystery is easily comprehended in a day when people are quick to announce the reality of angels and a belief in reincarnation.

However, Christianity cannot seize the day as long as it remains captive to a Western, rationalistic, institutionalized death grip that saps spiritual vitality. It must shed the old methods. It must step forward in courage and faith to experiment with different approaches. A new kind of postmodern music is playing. Can a church hear the new music and step to a different beat? Or will it ignore the spiritual moment and continue to dance the modern dance in a postmodern world?

Notes

[1]Jeff Gordinier, "On a Ka-ching! and a Prayer: In the Wake of 'Gump,' the Entertainment Industry Gets Spiritual and the Profits are Heaven-Sent," *Entertainment Weekly* 234, 7 October 1994, 36.

[2]George Hunter, *Church for the Unchurched* (Nashville: Abingdon Press, 1996) 23-24.

[3]Hans Christian Andersen, *His Classic Fairy Tales*, trans. Michael Foreman (New York: Doubleday,1974) 119-24.

[4]George Barna, *The Barna Report: What Americans Believe* (Ventura CA: Regal Books, 1991) 187.

[5]Barna, 184.

[6]Mike Regele, *Death of the Church* (Grand Rapids: Zondervan, 1995) 19.

[7]George Hunter, *Church for the Unchurched* (Nashville: Abingdon Press, 1996) 24.

[8]For a similar and historical perspective on "Plans of Salvation," see Ronald W. Johnson, *How Will They Hear If We Don't Listen? The Vital Role of Listening in Preaching and Personal Evangelism* (Nashville: Broadman and Holman, 1994) 48-56.

[9]George Barna, *Virtual America* (Ventura CA: Regal Books, 1994) 116.

[10]Andres Tapia, "Reaching the First Post-Christian Generation," *Christianity Today* (12 September 1994): 20-21.

[11]Abiel Abbot, "Traits of Resemblance in the People of the United States of America to Ancient Israel: In a Sermon Delivered at Haverhill, On the Twenty-eighth of November, 1799, The Day of Anniversary Thanksgiving. Haverhill, [MA], 1799," in *The American Republic and Ancient Israel*, ed. Moshe Davis (New York: Arno Press, 1977) 6.

The Dance

[12]See Robert N. Nash, Jr., "The Influence of American Myth on Southern Baptist Foreign Missions, 1845–1945" (Ph.D. thesis, Southern Baptist Theological Seminary, 1989), for a detailed analysis of the influence of the American mythology of divine chosenness on the growth of a major American Protestant foreign mission agency.

[13]Leander Keck, *The Church Confident* (Nashville: Abingdon Press, 1993) 38.

[14]Loren Mead, *The Once and Future Church: Reinventing the Congregation for a New Mission Frontier* (New York: The Alban Institute, 1991. 1994 ed.) 25.

[15]Leonard Sweet, *FaithQuakes* (Nashville: Abingdon Press, 1994) 109-110.

[16]Leander Keck, "The Premodern Bible in the Postmodern World," *Interpretation* 50, no. 2 (April 1996): 134.

[17]See Sweet, 48.

[18]Andraé Crouch, "Soon and Very Soon," in *The Baptist Hymnal* (Nashville: Convention Press, 1991) 192.

[19]Charles Wesley, "O For a Thousand Tongues to Sing," *in The Methodist Hymnal* (Nashville: Methodist Publishing House, 1966) 1.

[20]Dan R. Stiver, "Much Ado about Athens and Jerusalem: The Implications of Postmodernism for Faith," *Review and Expositor*, 91 (1994): 98.

[21]Karl Barth, *The Word of God and the Word of Men* (New York: Harper Torchbooks, 1957) 63. I borrowed extensively from Frederick Buechner's retelling of Barth's illustration in *Wishful Thinking: A Theological ABC* (New York: Harper & Row, 1973) 9.

[22]Frederick Buechner, *Wishful Thinking: A Theological ABC* (New York: Harper & Row, 1973) 53.

Chapter 4

The Tabernacle

The church is Christ's body
and is filled with Christ
who completely fills everything.
(Eph 1:23 CEV)

"What are all those people doing?" Tanya asked. Several students and I were standing in the middle of a shopping mall in Makati, a suburb of Manila. We had just completed a student/teacher exchange program in China and were spending a week in the Philippines. Directly in front of us, throngs of people pressed in around a kind of tabernacle structure.

It was open at the sides and rose above the shopping complex like an old revival camp meeting tent, except that it was a permanent building, supported by steel beams and covered by a tin roof. I could barely hear a preacher's voice rising above the din of honking Jeepney horns and noisy shoppers.

Our curiosity got the better of us, and we moved closer to the "tent" to see what was attracting so many people. Suddenly, music and singing replaced the preacher's voice. The chorus "Alleluia" lifted up over our heads and floated away in the night air. I felt peaceful and at home with the familiar music.

We edged even closer. The singing crowd parted a bit to let us through. A young priest dressed in traditional Catholic clerical garb stood in front of an altar that was covered with bread and wine. A woman stood behind him leading a series of praise choruses and hymns.

Soon the songs ended. The priest spoke again, moving effortlessly back and forth between English and Pilipino, the national dialect of the Philippines. "Come, Holy Spirit," he said. "Enter into our hearts this day that we might be your living vessels."

People in the crowd swayed back and forth. A few lifted their hands in acts of bodily worship. One or two spoke in tongues. The priest blessed the bread and the wine and pronounced it to be the body and blood of Jesus. Then he placed the bread upon the lips of the faithful.

I turned to look at a small bulletin board that contained announcements about the ministries and mission opportunities at the church. Bible studies and worship services and social ministries occurred on virtually every day of the week. A financial statement was posted. People were invited to write down their prayer concerns and place them in a small box.

The singing started again. Chills ran up and down my spine as I thought about the powerful witness of this church in its context. Here a community of Christians reached out to shoppers and beggars and taxi drivers and merchants. Here was a church without walls, a church that had essentially reinvented itself from the ground up.

People were free to stop by at their leisure, to eat lunch on a church pew, or to pray when the place was empty. The worship services served as a natural attraction as music and prayer and sermon beckoned weary shoppers to the sanctuary of the church.

Everything about the church seemed fluid. The open sides of the church invited people to enter its space whenever they needed a spiritual sanctuary. Its worship style implied an openness to many different forms of worship—to the traditional Catholic Eucharist or Lord's Supper, to the singing of heart music in the form of praise choruses, to Protestant hymns, to Pentecostal forms of prayer. The priest's effortless ability to move back and forth between the national dialect and English reflected the church's multifaceted ministry to many different nationalities of people.

Here people discovered a unique kind of community in the midst of a highly diverse and international culture. I could sense it. We were standing at the heart of a nation's financial and commercial district. And yet, despite the multicultural reality, people gathered for a common goal—to worship the God of Jesus Christ. I looked around at Filipinos, Americans, Europeans, other Asians, Protestants, and Catholics. Divisions melted away. In that church, we were "neither Jew nor Greek, slave nor free." We stood there as simply the church, united by that one indisputable reality.

I walked away with a warm glow in my heart. For a brief moment I had seen a vision of what the church could be. Perhaps my vision was only partially true. I am sure that this church overcame many challenges to reach the moment at which its life briefly intersected with mine. Another participant in that worship service might have come away with a completely different interpretation of the moment. But I am also sure that my ideas about the communal life of the church were forever changed by that event.

This open-air community church in Manila, Philippines, has seized upon the opportunities presented by a postmodern world. In this sense, it is "postmodern without being postmodernist."[1] It is postmodern because it has made a conscious decision to interact with the many cultures that surround it and to offer a place for community that is not limited by the usual ecclesiastical boundaries.

But it has not caved in to the postmodernist temptation to sacrifice the truth of the gospel. It stands unashamedly for that truth in a highly visible fashion. It offers an alternative way of worship and living that can hardly be ignored by anyone within hearing distance. Hundreds of passersby are attracted to it by its brand of spiritual community.

This church is a model for traditional churches in a postmodern world. I don't mean that every church should plant itself in the middle of a mall or shopping complex. And I certainly don't mean that churches should construct tabernacle-like sanctuaries without walls. I don't mean that every ethnic group ought to be represented in every church. But I do mean that this church should be emulated. Its ministries and worship attract postmodern people. And the nature of its community calls people beyond cultural barriers to a deeper unity.

The Postmodern Church
Toward a Definition

This congregation is a highly visible and alternative community of faith that follows the way of Jesus and is fully integrated into its surrounding culture. What a wonderful definition for the church! Does this definition fit your particular congregation? Churches are intended to be spiritual communions, "concerned with the whole life of humanity—spiritual, institutional, social, moral, and communal."[2] And yet most churches fall miserably short of this grand vision for the church. What makes this church in an Asian shopping complex such a wonderful metaphor for a postmodern church?

First, it is highly visible. Its visibility attracts people to it. They see it. They hear it. It does not apologize for calling people to the worship of Jesus Christ. It does not quietly undertake its worship and ministry task. This church speaks loudly and forcefully to the people whose eyes and ears fall within range of its witness.

I learned a valuable lesson as a nine-year-old about the power of Christian witness in the wider community. A young preacher took my grandfather (who was also a Baptist preacher) and me to lunch. When the food was served, the younger man said, "Why don't we each say our own individual blessings?"

My grandfather replied, "We will not! I don't pray quietly in public places!" And he proceeded to offer a loud prayer for the food. I opened one eye during his prayer and noticed that every single head in the restaurant was bowed!

Many traditional churches in the modern world are much too quiet. They carry on their spiritual obligations in such a way that few people see or hear their witness. Worship occurs behind walls. The gospel of Christ is rarely carried beyond those walls in any tangible way.

I once thought that such silence was forced upon a church by the secular world that surrounded it. Now I am convinced that many churches prefer to keep the walls up and the world out. It makes being church so much more simple.

Unfortunately, in a postmodern world, churches cannot be silent. They must insist upon being heard and seen. To be invisible is to be irrelevant. Silent churches will be relegated to obscurity. They will make no contribution to the communication of Christian faith in their communities.

Second, a church in the postmodern world must be grounded in the way of Jesus. Everything it does should emerge out of this voluntary submission. In the modern world, one could hardly distinguish a traditional church from a civic club or a country club. Postmodern churches will exist in a radically pluralistic world. They cannot afford such mistaken identity.

For this reason, postmodern churches must devote considerable time to understanding Christ's call to servanthood, to discipleship, and to self-sacrifice. Jesus called his disciples to live apart from possessions, to respond with love and concern for people on the margins of society, to turn the other cheek, to go the extra mile, and to love their enemies. In addition, they were to exhibit humility rather than power.

Stanley Hauerwas and William Willimon, co-authors *of Resident Aliens: Life in the Christian Colony,* offer a vision of the church as a colony of aliens in the world. This colony follows in the way of Jesus, a way characterized by engagement in political and social change as defined by the gospel of Jesus Christ. The church is to be a unique community, "shaped by a story of how God is with us."[3] The biblical story calls the church to reflect the gospel and to avoid cultural captivity.

Third, a church in the postmodern world must live out its life in an uneasy tension. It must be an alternative community of faith that is fully integrated into its surrounding culture.

It is easy to be an alternative community of faith. Such communities separate from the rest of the world. They live in a kind of vacuum. They make sure that they are so insulated from the world that none of its influence can reach them. At the same time, this separation virtually ensures that the church can have little impact on its culture. It is too removed to do anyone much good.

It is also easy for a church to be fully integrated into its surrounding culture. Most churches enjoy such integration. They mirror their particular context. The solid brick or wooden walls of most churches stand as visible symbols of the spiritual and communal walls that exist within the congregation. Community exists within such churches, but only for a select group of people who were raised in the church or who look very much like they could have been raised in the church. Such churches do not reflect the kind of community that ought to exist in the kingdom of God.

But it is difficult for a church to be both—to be an alternative community of faith that is fully integrated into its community. Such a church rises above race and class distinctions to mirror the inclusive kingdom of God. It also fully intersects its culture, penetrating to its very heart. Such penetration enables it to offer a glimpse into the kind of community that will exist in the kingdom of heaven. Such a church challenges its culture, rejoices with it, celebrates with it, and condemns it whenever necessary. But it never separates from it. It remains a vital and life-changing force within it that always influences it.

Becoming a Postmodern Community of Faith

What kind of community does my church need to become in a postmodern world? This is the question Christian congregations today must answer. One of the primary obligations of the church in any era is to offer a place of true community to people and to cultivate that community in such a way that it reflects the coming kingdom of God. The process of creating and cultivating Christian community is no simple feat. To accomplish this task, the church must ask itself three questions:

• What values exist within our congregation that distort Christian community?
• What kind of community attracts postmodern people?
• What kind of community reflects God's future kingdom?

The remainder of this chapter will focus upon some answers to these three questions. I hope my answers will stimulate your own reflections upon the kind of community offered by your congregation and the kinds of changes that might enhance that community.

What Distorts Christian Community?

The modern church is facing a "community" crisis among its membership. A recent Gallup poll reported that 80 percent of Americans believe that "individuals should arrive at their own religious beliefs *independent of any church or synagogue*" (italics mine).[4] James T. Richardson points to a new "social drift" model of conversion that now dominates the church scene in America.[5] Less than half of adult Americans remain in a single denomination throughout their lives.[6] They flit from one congregation to another without ever discovering the vital community they desperately crave.

Americans often convert several times in the course of their lives to a variety of Christian and non-Christian religious forms. Many of my childhood friends grew up in Southern Baptist churches, leaned heavily toward agnosticism in their twenties and thirties, dabbled a bit in Eastern religions, and are now either good Episcopalians or confirmed fundamentalists. They are likely to change again. No church or denomination ever captures their attention. No church community is good enough. The only constant in their lives is experimentation with various denominations and religions.

What has caused this religious rootlessness? Why do Americans drift from one church or denomination or religion to another? Many reasons exist. But I want to focus upon just one. Today's churches offer nothing unique. The community and spirituality they practice simply mirrors the wider culture. Traditional churches reinforce the values of American society. In partnership with schools and civic clubs, they offer an American way to be religious. They emphasize the values of America—efficiency, competition, power, and tradition—and soon become so entrapped in those values that they can offer little else.

In the process, the church loses its distinctiveness and flavor and distorts its community. In the Sermon on the Mount, Jesus called his followers to be like "salt for everyone on earth." And then he warned, "But if salt no longer tastes like salt, how can it make food salty? All it is good for is to be thrown out and walked on" (Matt 5:13 CEV). Churches are highly respected institutions in society. Church communities create and nurture solid citizens of the world. But they often fail to create and nurture "resident aliens" who reflect a higher order.

The American values of efficiency, competition, power, and tradition have each made a significant contribution to the life of the church. Churches focused upon efficient methods of church growth and evangelism that contributed to the rapid-fire spread of Christianity across the nation. Competition among those churches led to the rise of American denominations and the "churching" of a nation. Churches gained considerable power in American culture, enabling them to influence the nation's political and moral direction. American Christianity with its traditions of revivalism and denominationalism contributed to the common religious experience of the American people, providing identity and purpose.

But these values have now been distorted within most congregations. This distortion has led to a perverted gospel. This gospel rewards efficiency over ministry. It is characterized by a "win at all costs" mentality. It views power and prosperity as evidence of God's favor. It stubbornly clings to tradition and fears innovation. For these reasons, most American churches are nothing like the church I described at the beginning of this chapter. They offer nothing special. People look past them whenever they seek meaningful and unique spiritual communities. They represent the least exciting spiritual option in American religion.

Such perceptions will not go away as long as efficiency, competition, power, tradition, and other American cultural values hinder the spiritual and communal vitality of traditional churches. Consider the damaging effects of such values.

 Efficiency

I hadn't been long at a church when we had our first communion service. Admittedly, the service went a little long. My timing was not perfect. The bread and wine took a little bit longer to serve than I had anticipated. But I managed to wrap things up by about 12:08 on Sunday afternoon. And I felt quite good about how the day had gone. Or at least I felt good until I walked into the church office on Monday morning. A church member whom I had not yet met stopped me at the secretary's desk and introduced himself.

"Very nice to meet you, Mr. Jones," I said. I meant it. I was working doubly hard to get to know church members.

Ignoring my upbeat manner, Mr. Jones looked me straight in the eyes and said, "Did you know that you're a windbag?"

I was too stunned to offer much more than a quiet "I beg your pardon, sir?"

He quickly continued. "You're just gonna have to learn that we start services on time at this church and we end them on time. People expect that kind of efficiency."

Once I found my tongue, I managed to recommend a little book for his reading pleasure entitled *How to Win Friends and Influence People.* He desperately needed it!

Traditional churches are certainly efficient places. We take care to figure out the most efficient way to accomplish a task. To this end, we proclaim that churches ought to be run like businesses. We hire a corporate CEO called the pastor to oversee the place and to make sure that it runs efficiently. We begin and end our worship services on time. We insist that the business of the church be conducted in an orderly and efficient way.

This excessive emphasis upon efficiency quickly becomes a hindrance to ministry and community. Things must be done decently and in order. We cannot begin an afterschool program for children because of a lack of liability insurance. An act of the United States Congress is required to knock out the wall of a Sunday School class in order to make more room. The congregation cannot celebrate the addition of a new member into the church family until his/her decision is carefully recorded on a piece of paper. And, by all means, we must ask if there is any opposition to the decision (as if we have a choice about who belongs to God's community and who does not belong).

The church must become less interested in its own efficient operation and more concerned for the spiritual and communal needs of people. Who needs Robert's Rules of Order? Let's turn the church on its head by encouraging flexibility instead of conformity. Most traditional churches devote far more attention to programs than they devote to people. What if this tendency were reversed? Let's take a few church activities and imagine what such a reversal might accomplish.

Wednesday Night Fellowship Dinners. Many churches offer a Wednesday night fellowship dinner as a convenience to church members who are involved in prayer meeting, choir practice, and mission promotion activities. This meal provides a grand opportunity for the cultivation of friendships and the enhancement of church unity. And yet most churches insist upon wedging the supper in around a schedule chock full of programs. Church members rush to a 5:15 committee meeting, gulp down some iced tea and chicken, and then scramble to prayer meeting or to their responsibilities as a leader in a children's program. They return home exhausted, dreading the prospects of another Wednesday night.

By focusing upon people instead of programs, churches can dramatically change the flavor of a Wednesday night fellowship dinner. We eat meals for the sake of convenience. But we throw dinner parties for fellowship and conversation. For this reason, the fellowship dinner itself ought to be a dinner party thrown for the people of the church.

From this center hub, the congregation ought to move in and out through the evening, enjoying each other's company. Prayer ought to occur among the tables as each table group prays for itself, for the larger congregation, and for other concerns. Table talk should be encouraged. Church members can remain at the table or leave it for awhile to participate in an activity and return to it at leisure.

Church Committees. Most of you probably recoiled at the mere sight of these two little words. You're certainly in good company. Here is Leonard Sweet's assessment of church committees:

> A church dense with committees is a regatta of red tape that stands
> for unspiritual commitments, wasted time, unproductive hours,
> poor stewardship, and bored scribblings on the back of envelopes.[7]

He suggests that churches form ministry teams, roundtables, or other small groups that are created as a need arises and then dissolved once the need is met.

This organic approach to ministry has considerable merit. It deflects a church's attention from programs and organization to people and ministries. I recently participated in a small group discussion at a monthly deacon's meeting. Our task was to envision new staff alignments and new ministry approaches as our church looked toward the challenges of the twenty-first century. The very first person to speak suggested that we eliminate the committee structure of the church. No one voiced a word of protest!

Business Meetings. Nothing destroys church community quite like a business meeting. I dread them like the plague. Most church members show no interest in such meetings whatsoever. I can hardly blame them.

Business meetings are an extension of the committee structure of the church. They ensure that churches remain captive to an efficiency that saps spiritual energy.

Let's replace "business meetings" with a monthly or quarterly "family reunion" or "community mission and ministry review." Have a meal, or at least some cake and coffee. Celebrate with the new members who have joined the congregation. Send departing members off with a prayer for their ministry in a new congregation and a celebration of their contribution to the life of the church.

Invite the various ministry teams (remember, we no longer have church committees) to share ministry opportunities and future plans with the congregation. But don't call it a business meeting because that is not what it is! It is a celebration! It offers the chance for the church to consider its ministry to itself and to its community. It has nothing to do with business and everything to do with people and missions and ministry.

 ## Competition

Perhaps the efficiency of the modern church leads it to champion the cultural value of competition. Churches compete. They compete against themselves, and they compete against other congregations. They worry about what is happening at the church down the street. Pastors are particularly guilty of this sin. I know. I was once a pastor. I stood around at meetings with other pastors, jingled the change in my pockets, and compared statistics. I discussed ways to increase attendance at my church, making the assumption that increased attendance would solve all of the church's problems.

But pastors shouldn't bear all the blame. After all, increased attendance does solve many problems for a pastor. Congregations rate a pastor's performance by certain numerical criteria that they believe signals congregational health. They constantly compare their numerical accomplishments to those of neighboring churches.

Such competition is clearly evident in the huge Sunday School board that hangs over the entryway into the sanctuary from the Sunday School rooms or that is prominently displayed in the church bulletin. Huge black letters proclaim THE NUMBERS! Church members can quickly discern how the Sunday School attendance for the day stacks up against that of the previous Sunday and of the same Sunday in the previous year.

This competitive spirit leads to improper motivations. Numbers become an end-in-themselves instead of a means-to-an-end. We play all sorts of little games to increase THE NUMBERS. We "pack a pew" instead of offering a more meaningful service of worship that will attract people. We celebrate High Attendance Sunday as if high attendance is some sort of worthy goal. We forget that warm bodies in the Sunday School chair or in the pew mean absolutely nothing unless something meaningful occurs. We gauge success in the church by the number of people who attend and completely ignore more important questions such as, "How was our spirituality or community enhanced by this worship service or that Sunday School class?"

Competition can often destroy community. There is little purpose in it. It detracts from the idea that people should attend worship for worship's sake. And, perhaps more to the point, postmodern people are not motivated by the prospect of making the church look good. They do not attend worship in order to win a prize for the Sunday School class. They are quite straightforward with their reasons. There is something in it for them. Nothing is hidden. They come because they want to come. And if they want to stay home, they will do so. And no amount of begging, pleading, cajoling, or appealing to competitive pride can change their minds.

 Power

I recently took a look around the sanctuary of my own church. I noticed lawyers, financial analysts, city and county government officials, judges, doctors, professors, college presidents, corporate executives, bank presidents, and local school officials. It occurred to me that members of my local church were among the most powerful people in my town.

My church could do just about anything it wanted to do. Whenever it needed a loan, it could easily secure it. Government officials could probably be persuaded to vote on the side of an institution that included so many powerful people. It could probably get a street light placed at a certain intersection. It could exercise whatever amount of political, financial, or legal power it wanted to exercise. People would willingly cater to its every whim.

My church is not alone in its ability to wield such power. I have pastored small rural churches whose teachers and farmers and county agents harbored similar power within their communities. Such power is frightening and exhilarating all at the same time. It can be used for good, and it can certainly be used for ill.

Churches enjoy such power. They revel in it. It gives the church a kind of respectability in its community. It also gives it stability. Power brings comfort. It brings with it a sense of self-sufficiency. The church knows that if it is connected to the power structures of its society, then it can survive just about any trauma.

So what's wrong with being powerful? The problem with power is that churches rarely handle it very well. They tend to lose their way. Power becomes evidence of God's blessing. Power is not utilized to empower other people. Rather it is used to control others, to elevate the church in the eyes of the community, and to provide a power base from which to exercise control over the wider community. Humility takes a backseat to a new kind of sentiment that says, "We're first because God made us first!"

The kind of power that churches exercise in American culture today is a departure from the New Testament model for the church. Early Christian churches emerged at the edges of society and not at its power center. The powerful alliance between church and culture occurred only after Christianity was established as the official religion of the Roman empire. At first, the alliance benefited the church. But, in the end, the church lost its soul. It became little more than a tool of its culture, used when necessary to legitimate the operations of a secular government.

Nothing could be further from Jesus' intentions for the church. Traditional American churches can be helped to a new understanding of power by churches in non-Western contexts that often exist at the margins of society. Kwame Bediako, a Presbyterian theologian in Ghana, points out that "the essential character of Jesus' conception of power is that of power as non-dominating."[8] Philippians 2:10-11 clearly indicates that all creatures in heaven and earth "will openly proclaim that Jesus Christ is Lord" precisely because Jesus made himself of no account. He divested himself of power. Power comes through the sacrifice of power and not through the worldly exercise of it.

 Tradition

I recently led a Christmas Eve communion service for a congregation that had just called me as its interim pastor. Church members were so excited about the service. They told me about its simple beauty and reverence.

"I can't wait for you to experience it," said a young woman. "It just wouldn't be Christmas without it."

Everyone kept describing the how wonderful it would be. But no one seemed able to communicate to me, the leader of the service, exactly how it should be done. Whenever I asked for specifics, I was overwhelmed with general description and enthusiasm. Everyone knew exactly what to do but me.

I have never been so nervous in my life. I just knew that I was going to make a mistake. I even began the service with an apology. Then I jumped right in. Pew by pew and family by family, the members of that church made their way to the altar to receive communion. Each pew chose a leader to serve communion and to offer a prayer. It truly was one of the most beautiful and reverent services I have ever witnessed.

All congregations have their traditions. Traditions enhance community. Traditions provide stability. They are rather like old shoes that have been broken in and now wear quite comfortably. People enjoy rituals. They like to know that certain things will always remain the same. A healthy congregation must have certain good habits.

But traditions can often destroy community. Congregations can become so familiar with each other and so comfortable with their rituals and habits that they close their communities off to other people. Any innovation is viewed suspiciously. The seven last words of such a church are "We've never done it that way before."

In 1958, the College of Cardinals of the Roman Catholic church gathered in the Sistine Chapel to elect a new pope. They chose Angelo Giuseppe Roncalli, already seventy-seven years old, as a compromise candidate. Many cardinals assumed that he would be a pope of transition for a couple of years who would maintain the status quo. They would soon be surprised.

Roncalli assumed the name Pope John XXIII. In 1962, he convened the Second Vatican Council, a historic conference of the Roman Catholic Church that dramatically changed the traditions and direction of the Catholic faith. Vatican II transformed Catholicism forever. It permitted the Mass to be said in common languages instead of the traditional Latin. It acknowledged that laity were full participants in the mission of the church and could serve in baptism and confirmation. It advocated the use of new translations of the Bible that were based upon the original languages and encouraged personal Bible reading. It pronounced religious freedom to be a natural right.

As a result of Vatican II, Catholicism was freed from some of its captivity to tradition. Its structures were changed to reflect the realities of a new day. Today the Roman Catholic church is no longer a Western institution. It is arguably the world's most influential religious body. Its vitality is the direct result of its willingness to change its traditions and open itself up to new possibilities in a new day.

Traditional Protestant churches must engage in a similar process. Traditions will always make a vital contribution to church community. But the church now lives in an age in which traditions can destroy the ability of the church to transform itself and its structures. God is always doing something new. As postmodernity dawns, God needs a church that is open to new ideas, new worship styles, and new directions for ministry. God calls the church to become involved in the new thing God is doing.

A healthy congregation maintains a careful balance between tradition and innovation. It recognizes that new traditions are born out of creative moments in congregational life when the church insists upon doing a new thing. It also knows that its identity emerges from its traditions. Without them it loses its way.

But a word of caution is necessary. As churches move toward the twenty-first century, they had best err on the side of innovation. A congregation that insists upon traditional communal and spiritual forms must ensure that its motives are pure. Allegiance to tradition often betrays the existence of a siege mentality that would rather die in the fort than give up some ground. Christianity cannot tolerate many such churches. The future church will celebrate and affirm innovation, or it will die.

These four values—efficiency, competition, power, and tradition— shaped community in the modern American church. They will distort that community in the future unless churches have the courage to reduce their influence. These values reflect the points at which the American church has sacrificed its calling as an alternative community on the altar of cultural identity.

What Attracts Postmodern People?

The church has a responsibility to understand the communal needs of those people with whom it wishes to share the gospel of Jesus Christ. The church must ask the question, "To what kind of community are postmodern people attracted?" Once the church answers this question, then it must adjust its own structures to fit this new reality.

Community patterns of involvement have been significantly altered in recent years by such developments as television, computers, increased mobility, new work patterns, single parent and blended families, and larger urban populations. Let's look closely at these changes in order to understand how Americans now perceive community. In the past, denominations were important sources of community and commanded significant loyalty among the faithful. Group loyalties rarely wavered. Methodists remained Methodist. Baptists remained Baptist. Sometimes people did not switch "brands" even if they married someone of a different denomination.

Church membership served as a significant source of identity. People were assigned identities by the groups into which they were born. And they maintained these ascriptive or assigned loyalties until they died. This "brand" name loyalty significantly influenced the church. Churches didn't have to worry much about developing "community." People belonged to a church because they were born into it or at least into the larger "community" that surrounded it. They remained in that church for life. To join another church within fifty miles was to betray the "community." The church served as the center of social activity.

Families celebrated birthdays, reunions, and anniversaries in the fellowship hall and buried their loved ones in the church cemetery. In such a context, "community" occurred quite naturally. We went to church with our grandparents, parents, siblings, cousins, school buddies, and next-door neighbors. Community was easy. As the old saying goes, "You can choose your friends, but you can't choose your family."

Then that comfortable and traditional world went the way of all flesh. Young people got cars. They drove off to college. They took jobs in distant cities such as New York, Chicago, and San Francisco. Television came along, and then cable companies. We went from three channels to a hundred and three channels. Both spouses went to work to make ends meet. Little League baseball practice replaced farm chores. The family bought two cars. Soon "soccer moms" became a voting bloc. The old world passed away. A new world dawned.

In the end, traditional churches lost their place as the chief source of community for the American people. Church community suffered. People began to find community in places that had nothing to do with church. Self-help groups such as Alcoholics Anonymous, gender-specific groups such as Promise Keepers, sports groups such as the YMCA basketball league, and civic groups such as the Rotary Club provided at least as much community as a local church. And no one had to feel guilty about not attending church. After all, our "home" churches were usually far away in distant and often rural places. Community could be found in some other "club."[9]

Now traditional churches are trying to figure out what happened. Where did everyone go? Why did our children grow up, leave church, and never come home again? The answer is quite simple: Churches took "community" for granted. They thought it happened automatically. They didn't work at it because they didn't have to—at least they thought they didn't have to.

In 1994, shortly after my family and I moved to town, we began visiting churches in order to find one that felt like home. In the course of our search, we asked young couples to tell us why they chose their particular congregation.

One woman responded, "Well, we moved from California, and we were told that if you wanted to find community in the South, you needed to join a church."

Another person said, "Oh, we aren't really members. You see, we like the Sunday School class here and the preaching over at the Methodist church. So we come here first and then walk across the street for worship."

A young husband said, "This is really embarrassing! But we come here because it's the church I grew up in and, well, I guess we've just never looked anywhere else."

These responses provide evidence of a shift in the communal needs of the American public. They are marked by a peculiar absence of "brand" loyalty or at least an embarrassment that such "brand" loyalty should dictate one's participation in a church. I call it the "Super Wal-Martizing" of American Christianity. We go to the church that offers what we want for the least amount of trouble. Emerging Internet churches are more evidence of this trend. We can go to church in our bathrobes and slippers, hot coffee in hand.

Wade Clark Roof and William McKinney point to three trends in American Christianity that have had significant impact on patterns of church affiliation. First, Americans recovered a sense of the experiential in religion. They wanted something to happen at church. Second, emancipation of the self became a primary objective. They wanted whatever happened at church to happen to them and to make a difference in their lives. Finally, this new individualism led to the perception that institutions should serve people and not vice versa.[10] Churches were useless unless they contributed something meaningful to people's lives.

These trends help to explain why some people join a particular church when others do not. Personal fulfillment has become much more important than self-sacrifice as a reason for joining a religious group. People now have a passionate hunger for personal experience.[11] We explored this hunger in the third chapter. It holds certain implications for the formation of Christian community.

It signals that a new brand of individualism has emerged in American culture. Today's prospective church member wants to know, "What's in it for me?" We can protest that such an attitude is selfish. We can preach sermons on self-sacrifice and insist that the church is a place in which we are to give without counting the cost. But the reality remains. People will not participate in a church unless it offers something to them in return for their participation.

Churches cannot change this new brand of "me-ness." Individualism rests at the heart of Western culture. It was born in the Enlightenment emphasis upon the worth of the individual person. It was fueled by the ideas of Martin Luther who insisted that all believers were priests and had the right to go directly before God with their sins and concerns. Baptists contributed to it with their notions of soul competency and religious liberty. American revivalists insisted upon the cultivation of a "personal" relationship with Christ. Americans were weaned on individualism. They aren't likely to get over it anytime soon.

Just a moment ago I indicated that, in the modern world, our communities were assigned to us. We were born into them and remained attached to them for the bulk of our lives. We were born a Baptist or a Democrat, and we stayed that way. But in a postmodern world, we choose the communities with which we will affiliate.

Postmodern people expend a great deal of energy to answer the question, "Who am I?" They work to establish personal identity. The recent proliferation of self-help books and seminars are an indication of this emerging concern for personal identity. Once identity is established, then postmodern people seek out those community affiliations that will nurture their personal identities.

Churches must take into account this volatile mix of individual and community needs. The key word congregations must keep in mind is "choice." Postmodern people have a choice, and they celebrate this freedom to choose. Robert Wuthnow warns that

> church leaders are simply deluded if they think people . . . are desperately seeking a "community" with which to associate and will attend church in hopes of finding it there.[12]

Postmodern people do not need community. In fact, they have all the community they can stand. Their community needs are met at PTO meetings, Rotary Clubs, conversations with other soccer moms, supper clubs, and a variety of other communal connections. Church is simply one more choice in a cafeteria line of community opportunities.

So what should the church do in light of this emphasis upon individualism if it is to attract postmodern people?

Today's church must find its niche.

We recently moved away from a dying town. Several years before our arrival, Wal-Mart attempted to build a store there. Local business leaders refused to allow it. They gathered enough political clout to keep Wal-Mart out. Of course, Wal-Mart immediately built a store in another town about twenty miles away. And the new Wal-Mart, along with other local businesses, became a hub for shopping.

People drove from our small dying town to the now-bustling other town with its new Wal-Mart. Our town continued to die. The other town was reborn. Business owners diversified. They adjusted their inventory to fill consumer needs that Wal-mart couldn't meet. Some merchants sold antiques. Others sold more expensive lines of clothing or shoes. Nearly everyone survived. And the town was better off for it.[13]

I once ministered in a medium-sized church that was located about a half-mile from the fastest growing congregation in town. This megachurch had everything! It was a Wal-Mart in itself! It had a dynamic preacher, a huge staff of ministers, wonderful worship services, a health club, a day care, and a swimming pool. Its resources attracted thousands of people to it.

My little church developed an inferiority complex. After all, we were just the little church on the corner with our traditional worship service and our traditional programs. We stared in awe at the big church down the street. We asked ourselves, "What makes us special?" At first, we were perplexed. Then it occurred to us. There were many people who liked the small, intimate kind of community that existed at our traditional Baptist church. We couldn't offer health club memberships or provide day care. But we could certainly provide people with a community of faith where "everybody knows my name." And that's exactly what we set out to do.

Churches must discover their unique little niches. Their survival depends upon it. What makes your church unique? What human need does it meet that would otherwise go unmet? Your church might have a reputation as a conservative or fundamentalist congregation. Everyone in town knows that your church stands for the rights of the unborn child and works diligently to recover the right to pray in public schools. This is your niche. Cultivate it.

You might belong to a progressive congregation that is known for its support of women in ministry. Everyone in town knows that you sanction the ordination of women to service as deacons and pastors. This is your niche. It will attract many people into your community of faith. Cultivate and nurture this distinction. It sets you apart.

A church must find a niche and fill it. Its unique mission and purpose as a congregation will attract people with similar concerns. They will choose to belong to a congregation because its ministries and worship style square nicely with their own hopes and dreams for the church. They have chosen their church, and this freedom of choice will create intense loyalty and unbridled enthusiasm.[14]

 Today's church must localize its identity.

Individualism in American Christianity is revitalizing ministry on the local level. The early twentieth century witnessed the emergence of denominational boards and agencies that were "powered by a strong clear uniform paradigm of mission."[15] This single denominational vision is evaporating. It is being replaced by the realization that a church's mission field begins at its front door.

Denominations are losing their hold on American Christians. In fact, denominational tags today are becoming much like school mascot names—interesting, but relatively insignificant.[16] The local church is the heart of religious life. It is moving increasingly toward local affiliations, local mission projects, and local community ministry organizations. And it is moving away from denominational connections.

Nancy Ammerman predicts that the organizational structure of the church will be much more decentralized and democratic in the future, with increased autonomy:

> If efficiency was the watchword of the 1920s, participation may be today's watchword. . . . Each congregation will assess its own needs and resources, seeking the particular set of organizational connections called for by their sense of mission.[17]

Many businesses advocate shared leadership that provides autonomy to each separate working unit. Supervisors no longer hand decisions down to employees. Instead, teams of employees take a problem and solve it.

In the words of a popular bumper sticker, congregations are beginning to "think globally and act locally." Such local participation will create a greater sense of community in local congregations. Churches can determine the niche they want to fill and seek out those denominational and community organizations that will help them to fill that niche.

The good news is that postmodern people want to know that they are making a difference in their local communities. They want to participate in organizations that are working for change. They want to get their hands dirty. They want to see the visible results of their labors. Localized ministry makes a church a highly attractive place from which to work for the betterment of society.

 Today's church must let leadership "trickle up."

This process of localization is empowering church members to once again take an active role in the mission and ministry of the church. Harvey Cox observes:

> Whereas once theology was manufactured at the center for distribution in the provinces, the direction of the flow is being reversed. It is the periphery that is now threatening, questioning, and energizing the center.[18]

A kind of "hands-on" involvement in church leadership is emerging. Postmodern church members want to be involved in decision-making processes, small group ministries, worship leadership, and mission opportunities. Recent experiences with deacon chairpersons in two different churches have borne out this transition.

The deacon chairperson at my own church has emerged as a visionary congregational leader. He has played a vital role in empowering lay leadership and has insisted upon the implementation of a church mission statement and goals. His powerful influence is revitalizing the church. He attends ministry conferences with the ministers and has assumed a lay ministry role in the church. Other members of the congregation are following his lead.

The deacon chairperson at the church where I serve as an interim pastor has fulfilled a similar function. He continued to serve as the worship leader of the congregation for several weeks after I assumed my pastoral duties. I thoroughly enjoyed his obvious talents in creating a proper worship environment and hoped that he would continue in this vital ministry. But he gave up the job after several church members expressed the desire that I should fulfill these duties. Despite my protests, he insisted upon a less visible role.

This "trickle-up" approach to ministry signals an exciting transition in American Christianity. Historically, Protestant congregations have entrusted clergy with the primary responsibility for shaping the missions and ministry structures of the church. The denomination provided programs and a common vision for the churches that were loosely tied to it. Denominational spokespersons preached the benefits of cooperation. Denominational seminaries shaped young ministers into denominational loyalists. Denominational bureaucracies stood ready to offer assistance whenever congregations needed advice on fund-raising, choosing a pastor, or writing a church history.

Now church members want hands-on involvement. And this desire can rejuvenate the local church. It can free professional clergy to become equippers and encouragers. It can enable the church to become a team with a common purpose and identity that emerge from shared ministry. It can create considerable personal investment on the part of the laity in the future direction of the congregation. But it will require active listening on the part of professional ministers. Ideas for ministry, worship, and missions will "trickle-up," and clergy will be faced with a rather confusing array of ministry hopes and dreams to which they must give direction.

 Today's church must empower its members.

On a recent class trip to a Jewish synagogue, one of my students asked the rabbi if the synagogue often took in new members.

The rabbi responded, "Sometimes a non-Jew will stop me after a service and tell me that he wants to become a Jew. I say to him, 'What! Are you crazy? Why would anyone want to be a Jew? Do you know what happens to Jews? Jews die. Other people hate them. Get out of here!' "

He continued. "Some of these people will return again. And they will say that they really do want to be Jewish. I shoo them away again.

"But if they come a third time, then I think that maybe they really do want to become a Jew. And I begin to talk with them about what this means and that the process of becoming Jewish is long and arduous."

What would happen if a church's pastor responded in a similar fashion to a prospective church member?

"What!? Are you crazy? Why would you want to join this church? Do you want to spend your life at the end of the line or sell all you have and give it to the poor? Do you really want to love your enemies? Get out of here! You don't really want to be a member here!"

It will never happen. Christian churches rarely focus on the qualities that distinguish them from the rest of the world. They prefer to let people discover these truths for themselves in the context of personal quiet time. Perhaps this is why churches often take people into their communities and then leave them to fend for themselves.

This kind of abandonment seems to be a unique feature of American churches. It rarely occurs in the synagogues of Judaism or the mosques of Islam. And it cannot continue to happen in the church. New community members must be empowered with the stories and traditions of a local church and the nature of its missions and ministries. The unique demands of the Christian life must be made clear to them.

Now local church identity supersedes that of the national or state denomination. People choose a church because it meets their particular needs. They recognize that their decision is a significant one that places certain obligations upon them. They do not have to join a church at all. Yet, they have still chosen to do so.

This reality places an obligation upon the church to empower its membership for effective service. New church members must be integrated into the life of the community through a careful process. This process should enable them to discover their own place in the body of Christ. It should introduce them to the story of the congregation, to the ministries of the church, to its vision, and to their obligations as participants in it.

New members ought to be assigned community partners who are familiar with the congregation and who can assist with developing personal relationships and connecting interests and spiritual gifts with ministry opportunities. It might be a good idea to organize orientation groups composed of both new members and old members. Persons who have a lengthy history in the church can serve as encouragers and equippers for the empowerment of new church members. Such groups become conduits into the wider fellowship of the church family.

But a church must also empower its entire membership with the theological and practical skills that are essential for effective ministry. Lay ministry is emerging as a new model for church life. Trends now indicate a sharp reduction in charitable contributions to the church. Fewer professional clergy will be hired. Lay ministers will become increasingly valuable to local churches. But these lay ministers will not attend seminaries. They will receive their training in the church. Congregations must be prepared to provide theological and practical education in ministry.

The good news is that a new kind of church can now be born out of the ashes of the old traditional community church. This new church stands a better chance of reflecting the coming kingdom of God precisely because community will not be handed to it on a silver platter. Its members will choose to join it; they will not be born into it. Its mission and purpose will be more sharply defined because its reasons for existence will rest in the future and not in the past.

What Kind of Community Reflects God's Kingdom?

Coach Mullins, my high school cross-country coach, had a little motor scooter he putt-putted around on to encourage us during practice. He loved to ride up behind us while we were running the 3.2-mile course and try to motivate us to run even faster.

One day he pulled alongside me and said, "Nash, you're slowing down. What's wrong?"

"Don't worry, coach!" I huffed. "I'll make it to the finish line."

He looked at me with considerable disdain, as if I were a glass of sour milk. "Making it to the finish line isn't the point!" He said. "The point is to get better every time you run."

Most churches are content to simply get to the finish line. They really don't care much whether they run a good race. They have settled into a nicely-paced gait that they believe will eventually carry them across the line and into the future kingdom of God. It is enough for them!

But it is not enough for God. God expects the church to be more than simply a community that attracts people to it by adjusting itself to fit human needs and desires. Glenn Hinson once challenged the church "to fashion a heavenly citizenry who can show forth the true end and purpose of humanity."[19] Such a church must shape and form among its membership the kind of alternative community expected of it by Jesus Christ. This kind of community calls church members beyond themselves and their own selfish community needs and toward a deeper form of community.

Such community is not self-serving; it is Christ-centered. It is absolutely unattainable because it is grounded in selfless love and concern and is extended from one member of the community to another without concern for race, gender, social status, economic level, or any other cultural restriction. The church cannot consistently reflect such a community. But even the slightest evidence of it is infectious.

The church of Jesus Christ is unique among all other institutions and communities of the world. It offers the only hope on earth for true community. It has an obligation to call people beyond individualism, efficiency, power, competition, self-help seminars, and tradition and drag them kicking and screaming toward the kingdom of God. It must strive to accomplish this task even if failure is inevitable. It must run well. It must do much more than simply put one foot in front of the other.

This endeavor requires a church to dream about what it ought to be. Such dreams are rooted in the gospel of Jesus Christ. Such dreams create tension in the body. Such dreams cause pain and hurt as muscles adjust to greater levels of exertion and a faster pace. Such dreams can never be satisfied with the way things are but must look with hope toward a future that is as yet unrealized.

Such churches call people beyond their individuality and toward meaningful community. Stanley Grenz argues that "postmodern evangelicals must carry out a theology that integrates the human person into community."[20] The kingdom of God is a communal kingdom. It is not a place where individual needs and desires hold sway. It is a place in which the needs and desires of the entire community are satisfied by a single well of water that moistens all parched throats.

People need this particular kind of community. They need a community that offers a grand reason for human existence, a community that calls them to selflessness and sacrifice. If persons are embedded in such a community, then it can serve as the center from which they make sense of their lives. It should be more than just one of the many things they do. It should be the community out of which and for which they do everything.

Such churches encourage their members to risk diversity. I recently found myself in a three-way conversation over why African-Americans and Anglo-Americans usually worship in separate churches.

"We both prefer our own worship styles," insisted one person.

"But what we prefer isn't always what God prefers," said the other.

She was right! Churches celebrate sameness, not diversity. H. Richard Niebuhr once said that "Christendom has . . . achieved apparent success by ignoring the precepts of its founder." He called denominationalism a compromise between the church and the world.[21]

His words are worth hearing again. The gospel condemns the building up of walls that destroy community. Jesus denounced class distinctions and insisted upon the full participation of Samaritans, lepers, prostitutes, and tax collectors in the kingdom of God. Paul condemned theological divisions among the followers of Jesus, Paul, Apollos, and Peter. He also insisted that no distinction should exist in the church between Jew and Greek, male and female, slave and free.

Churches must risk diversity. That diversity should include the full family of faith—Asians, Americans, blacks, whites, conservatives, liberals, rich, and poor. Such diversity is uncomfortable. It cuts against the grain. It calls the church beyond walls and toward the full communion of the saints. Anything less than this full communion is contrary in spirit to the gospel of Christ.

And finally, such churches must return to their biblical roots to rediscover God's dreams for the church. Churches cannot be true communities of faith until they hold themselves accountable to the gospel. Let's face it. Most traditional churches do not reflect the gospel at all. Their sights are set much too low. Their cultural values have them by the throat. They can hardly breathe. They gasp for fresh air and have no idea where to go for it.

A group of churches does exist whose brand of community is quite close to the kind of church community called for in the Bible. But these churches exist in places to which traditional American churches rarely direct their attention. They are found mostly in Africa, Asia, and South and Central America. In fact, the Christians in these churches now outnumber Christians in Europe and North America by almost one third.[22]

This change in Christianity's center of gravity occurred just in the nick of time. Christianity would be in serious trouble today if traditional American churches were its most vital center. The American South is no longer the Bible Belt. That belt now stretches from Pentecostal churches in sub-Saharan Africa to house churches in China to tabernacle-style structures in Manila shopping malls. Traditional American churches must turn to these churches for renewal of spirit and community and a recovery of biblical faith.

We have much to learn from them. They offer powerful models for Christian community. They are rooted in the gospel and dedicated to creating communities of equality that mirror the future kingdom of God. These churches exist on the margins of society. They are New Testament churches in the purest sense of the word, for they are places of radical equality that fight dehumanization and economic deprivation and call people to salvation in Jesus Christ.[23]

I know a young Chinese woman named Christa who is a member of just such a New Testament church, a house church deep in the heart of China. She lives in the world's new Bible Belt. I first met Christa at a train station in Luoyang, a city in Henan Province in the People's Republic of China. Some students and I had traveled there to see the famous Longmen Caves that contain thousands of Buddhas of different shapes and sizes. Despite a torrential rain and an hour-long train delay, she was glad to welcome five native English speakers from the deepest part of the American South.

As soon as we were in the van, she asked a sudden and startling question.

"Are you Christians?" she inquired.

"Uh, yes, we are," I blurted out.

"Me too." She said. "The pastor who baptized me gave me the English name Christa at my baptism. It means Christ, you know."

We sat in silence for a moment.

"I know a song," she said. And she began to sing.

I expected John Denver's "Almost Heaven, West Virginia," which nearly every Chinese seems to know. What I heard instead was a beautiful soprano voice singing, "God is so good, God is so good, God is so good, He's so good to me."

We all joined in the singing. Later, we listened as Christa told us of her house church. She talked of its care and support of her and of the way in which the members of the church had raised her in the Christian faith. We learned that Christa was in the middle of praying over a very serious decision. The pastor of her house church, a Korean woman, had been forced to flee the country just ahead of deportation. Christa had been asked to fill the vacancy.

As the van moved through the streets of Luoyang and the rain streamed down the windows, I thought of the great spiritual decisions with which I had wrestled over the past few months. Do I have time to teach that Sunday School class next Sunday? Should I continue to serve on the church history committee? Where will I eat Sunday dinner today? Maybe I'll take my name off that deacon nomination list.

And then it occurred to me. Maybe there was something to be said for a community of faith that lived life on the edge. I wondered what it would cost for me—and for my church—to move there.

Notes

[1]Gene Edward Veith, *Postmodern Times: A Christian Guide to Contemporary Thought and Culture* (Wheaton IL: Crossway Books, 1994) 210.

[2]Bill J. Leonard, *The Nature of the Church* (Nashville: Broadman Press, 1986) 13.

[3]Stanley Hauerwas and William Willimon, *Resident Aliens: Life in the Christian Colony* (Nashville: Abingdon Press, 1989) 30.

[4]Jack Wertheimer, *A People Divided: Judaism in Contemporary America* (New York: BasicBooks, 1993) 191.

[5]James T. Richardson, "Studies of Conversion: Secularization or Re-enchantment," in *The Sacred in a Secular Age*, ed. Phillip E. Hammond (Berkeley CA: University of California Press, 1985) 110.

[6]Wertheimer, 191.

[7]Leonard Sweet, *FaithQuakes* (Nashville: Abingdon Press, 1994) 170.

[8]Kwame Bediako, "Jesus in African Culture: A Ghanian Perspective," *in Emerging Voices in Global Christian Theology* (Grand Rapids: Zondervan, 1994) 109-110.

[9]See Robert Wuthnow, *Sharing the Journey: Support Groups and America's New Quest for Community* (New York: The Free Press, 1994).

[10]Wade Clark Roof and William McKinney, *American Mainline Religion: Its Changing Shape and Future* (New Brunswick NJ: Rutgers University Press, 1987) 49-50.

[11]Martin E. Marty, "Transpositions: American Religion in the 1980s," in *Annals of the American Academy of Political Science*, 480 (July 1985): 20-21.

[12]Robert Wuthnow, *Christianity in the Twenty-First Century: Reflections on the Challenges Ahead* (New York: Oxford University Press, 1993) 51.

[13]Sweet, 112.

[14]Wertheimer, 44-45.

[15]Loren Mead, *The Once and Future Church: Reinventing the Congregation for a New Mission Frontier* (New York: The Alban Institute, 1991. 1994 ed.) 3.

[16]Wuthnow, 28.

[17]Nancy T. Ammerman, "After the Battles: Emerging Organizational Forms," in *Southern Baptists Observed: Multiple Perspectives on a Changing Denomination*, ed. Nancy T. Ammerman (Knoxville TN: University of Knoxville Press, 1993) 12.

[18]Harvey Cox, *Religion in the Secular City: Toward a Postmodern Theology* (New York: Simon and Schuster, 1984) 175.

[19]E. Glenn Hinson, *The Integrity of the Church* (Nashville: Broadman Press, 1978) 179.

[20]Stanley J. Grenz, "Star Trek and the Next Generation: Postmodernism and the Future of Evangelical Theology," in *The Challenge of Postmodernism: An Evangelical Engagement*, ed. David S. Dockery (Wheaton IL: Victor Books, 1995) 98-99.

[21]H. Richard Niebuhr, *The Social Sources of Denominationalism* (New York: Henry Holt & Co., 1929. 1975 edition) 1, 6-7.

[22]William Dyrness, ed., *Emerging Voices in Global Christian Theology* (Grand Rapids: Zondervan, 1994) 10. In 1992, 974.3 million Christians lived in the third world, compared to 600.8 million in western countries.

[23]Priscilla Pope-Levison and John R. Levison, *Jesus in Global Contexts* (Louisville KY: John Knox Press, 1992) 35.

Conclusion

God's New Church

Forget the former things;
Do not dwell on the past.
See, I am doing a new thing!
Now it springs up;
Do you not perceive it?
(Isa 43:18-19 CEV)

Like many fathers today, I witnessed the births of my children. I stroked my wife's face in the labor and delivery room, wiped her sweat, encouraged her along, timed her contractions, and did all those other "helping" tasks that have become a regular part of paternal childbirth responsibilities.

I remember quite clearly the experience of holding my oldest child, a newborn daughter, in my arms. A nurse captured the moment on film. My eyes, framed by a yellow surgical cap and mask and crinkled at the corners by a smile, squint proudly up at the camera. My daughter is obviously unhappy. Her journey through the birth canal had roughed her up a bit. Her head, slightly misshapen by the suction cup, is twisted with fury.

I couldn't tell much about her. I had no idea what she might someday look like. Would she be tall? Short? Would she enjoy throwing a baseball or playing a piano? Would there be a stubborn streak in her like her great-grandfather Nash? Would she prefer the thrill of the stage or the quiet refuge of a good book?

I only knew that I finally held her in my arms. And that time would soon enough offer up the answers to all of my questions. Something of what she would become depended upon me and upon others who would influence her life. Something of it depended upon her alone. And some of it was simply predetermined.

The birthing process would take years. In time, a personality would emerge. For the next few years, her mother and I would be midwives in the creation of this new personality, pushing here and encouraging there. She would have her own ideas of who she should be, and, together with grandparents and friends and siblings, we would nurture her dreams, at least as long as she would let us.

God is birthing a new church. And we Christians at the end of the twentieth century are rather like prospective parents awaiting its birth. Loren Mead says that "we are . . . midwives for a new church, working to help our present forms and structures give birth to forms appropriate for the new mission of the church."[1] We do not know exactly what such a church will look like. But we do know that it will be very much different from the churches to which most of us now belong. On occasion we catch a glimpse of it—in a communion service, at a Manila shopping center, during a Sunday School class, when we embrace a stranger.

Sometimes we are reluctant participants in its birth. But that is to be expected. Nothing upsets the apple cart quite like a brand new addition to the family! Everyone has to make some adjustments. Sleep is disturbed. Arguments ensue. Family traditions are upset. It takes years for anything resembling stability to reassert itself. But one thing is certain. There is no returning to the good old days when one had time to read the paper and drink a quick cup of coffee.

Many people are still skeptical. They really do not believe that such dramatic change must occur within the church. They are quite confident that the old church, with its revivals, quarterly communion services, committee structures, business meetings, and battles between traditionalists and progressivists will do just fine. They prefer to stay the course. They hold on to the dream that one day things will be set aright. They want nothing to do with birthing a new church.

This book has sounded a warning. Traditional American churches no longer have a choice. Change must occur, for death is inevitable. In a matter of years, traditional churches will disappear. Some of them will die quite natural deaths from old age. They will reach the stage of life at which their bodies can no longer cope with the demands of daily existence. They will quietly fade into oblivion. Those who observe their deaths will say, "They lived good lives. They did much good with the time allotted to them."

These traditional churches certainly made invaluable contributions to God's kingdom. They nurtured a kind of faith that enabled the church to find its way to the very center of American life. Its forms of revivalism and evangelism served as a vital entryway for millions of Americans who discovered Jesus Christ in the context of a traditional American church.

But then they became enslaved to old forms. They ignored the new things God was doing. They were rather like the church of the Middle Ages that just failed to see a new world dawning. They thought that they were strong, but they were really quite weak. They stood proudly on street corners and along rural highways. But they turned out to be nothing more than a façade, a Hollywood movie set that was built to look like something of substance and then was quickly dismantled. They died because they could not change.

Some traditional churches will choose a different kind of death. In my estimation, it is the better choice. They will stand at the same crossroads. They will look at the choices that are available to them. They will notice that they have become islands in the sea of a changing world. Their walls now protect a brand of old-time religion that makes no contribution at all to the lives of the people who live in the shadows of their fortresses.

They, too, will die. But their deaths will be of a different sort. The Christians within their walls will understand the difference between the church as a cultural institution and the church as an alternative community of faith fully integrated into its surrounding culture. These Christian people will become midwives for a new church.

The old church will slowly be laid to rest, but its death will make way for the new church that will emerge in its place. Its bricks and boards will be disassembled. And a new church will gradually be born. The bricks that divided the church from the world will be buried deep in the ground. A new roof will be laid over a church that now has no walls. Its music will slowly begin to drift out over the world that surrounds it. The old church will pass away, and the new church will be born in its place. This traditional church will leave something behind to carry on its mission in a new day.

Why will traditional churches die? Indeed, why must they die? This book has offered many reasons. Let me review the three major ones.

A new postmodern world has been born.

This postmodern world is the fish bowl in which all traditional churches now swim. It is a world of easy belief, a world in which people are quick to put their faith in reincarnation and nirvana and to find meaning in self-help books and wholistic health. It is a world in which many people doubt the existence of an absolute truth. Their truth is simply their truth. No one else has to believe it. In fact, other people have every right to live out their own particular brands of truth.

Truth is relative in such a world. Various kinds of truth compete for attention. People doubt that any single truth exists. They insist that the Christian brand of truth is culturally shaped and conditioned and that Christians believe it because they were raised in it. For this reason, Christianity is unable to rise above the many other realities that compete against it. It becomes simply one among many faiths that can provide meaning to human existence. No longer do people believe that one's eternal destination hangs in the balance. Other religions offer different realities with sharply differing views of the afterlife.

These realities are difficult to refute. Millions, even billions, of people around the world accept them. Some religions are much older than the Christian faith. Christianity barely holds its own in competing against them. Islam now has more than a billion adherents and is the fastest growing faith in the United States. Hinduism and Buddhism are hardly less vital.

In desperation, Christianity attempts to legitimate itself on the playing field of human reason. It forgets that its notions of truth require the same faith leaps as any of these other traditions. The only proof of its vitality rests in its ability to offer meaning to the lives of the Christian faithful. And the only way to make it more attractive is for its adherents to live out its story in such a way that other people also desire to experience it. For this reason, a new kind of Christian church must emerge in a postmodern world.

Most traditional churches in their present form are insufficient for the task of enhancing spirituality and Christian community in a postmodern world.

Traditional churches were built to order for the modern world of rationalism and science. They grew up in a context in which the Christian faith was the only available form of spiritual truth. Science was its sole competition. In that old modern world, churches constructed elaborate defenses of Christianity and the Bible in order to combat science. Science won the war, and, in time, Christians raised the white flag of surrender.

Traditionalist and progressivist Christians alike constructed modern churches that were monuments to common sense and reason. Traditionalists insisted that scientific discoveries proved the truth of the Bible. They turned the Bible into a rational and propositional prooftext of reality. They proved the Christian Story, and, in the process, they ripped the supernatural heart right of it. They built a propositional form of Christianity that rewarded proper doctrine over a living and vital experience with God.

Progressivists did the very same thing. They elevated human intellect and devalued the Bible. They insisted that the Bible conform to the emerging scientific discoveries of the day. They viewed scientific truth as ultimate truth. Biblical truth was somehow secondary to this highest form of truth. What couldn't be explained was simply explained away. Both groups seriously undermined the ability of the biblical story to inform the lives of people.

Then postmodernity dawned. Science became the least of the church's worries. Now it had to compete with other religions. People no longer sought scientific proof for faith. They found spiritual meaning in angels and goddesses and scented candles and yoga. Traditional churches were trapped. They had built the church around the idea of a single truth that would be obvious to anyone who cared to adopt it. They had sacrificed the souls of their churches upon the altar of a scientific worldview.

The tasks of spiritual nurture and the cultivation of Christian community had taken a backseat to proving the faith. Belief first, meaning second. This was the order of priorities of traditional modern churches.

There was no need to enhance spirituality and community in this life. These categories took second place behind proper belief.

Traditional churches were places of safety, in which one's right beliefs kept one from the fires of hell. Christians celebrated their survival of a close call and did their best to pull other people into the lifeboat. But there was little reason to offer meaningful spirituality and community that would enhance one's life in this world. It was much more important to ensure correct belief in order to provide a safety net in the next world.

The postmodern world reversed these two priorities. Meaning became much more important than proper belief. People wanted a faith that enhanced life in this world and that offered spiritual meaning for human existence. Instead, the church offered a set of doctrines that must be believed if one's existence was to continue in the next world. Christian faith was rooted not in meaningful living, but in believing the right things.

But postmodern people wanted so much more. Commitment to the church declined. Some people left religion behind altogether. Others discovered new religious forms that were much more vitally meaningful than the brand of Christianity proffered at traditional churches. Some merged their newfound faiths with their Christian lives, drawing from a wide range of spiritual sources. Others maintained a loose connection with the church in order to ensure their place in heaven. The church failed in its primary obligations. It failed to nurture Christian spirituality among its members. It also failed to establish a community of faith on earth that reflected the future kingdom of God in heaven. It was insufficient to the task.

 A new church must now be born.

I recently gathered on a cold Sunday morning with a group of children who ranged in age from about eight to twelve years old. New believers in Jesus Christ, they would soon be baptized into the Christian family. The church had asked that I assist them in understanding the significance of the step they were about to take.

We talked about salvation and church, water, and the cross, and then I asked them a "what if?" question:

"What if you went to a store with your mom or dad, and in that store you saw a toy that you really wanted? And you knew that you could put that toy under your coat and walk out of the store and no one would ever know that you had taken it? Would you take it?"

Everyone's head shook furiously. Resounding choruses of "No's!" nearly bowled me over.

"Why not?" I asked.

"God doesn't want me to," said one boy.

"It would be stealing," said another.

A shy young girl raised her hand. I nodded my head for her to speak.

"Because Jesus loves the people in the store," she said.

"Yes," I said. "That's it. Jesus loves the people who own the store. And because Jesus loves them, we love them, and we cannot do anything to hurt them."

I went on to say that everything we do as followers of Jesus Christ is done because Jesus loves us. Most people in the world know that stealing is wrong. But only Christians make it a point not to steal "because Jesus loves the people in the store."

This young child offered a wonderful insight that all Christian people must understand if the church today is going to survive. God's future church must live out of the grand Christian Story that is centered in Jesus Christ. This is the reason for its existence. It does not exist to enforce moral laws that are already obeyed by many non-Christian people in the world. It exists to live its life under the Lordship of Christ. Christian people don't steal for the simple reason that one can't steal and follow Jesus all at the same time.

Jesus oozes from the pores of the church. This is the great Truth that is proclaimed in the Scriptures: "The church . . . is his [Christ's] body. The fullness of him who fills all in all" (Eph 1:23). The problem that confronts the church today is that too many other reasons now dictate why it does the things it does. It is no longer saturated with Christ. It conducts business in order to operate efficiently. It worries too much about how its actions will be perceived by its community. It devotes its energy to programs instead of people. It oozes with the sweat of its own brow.

But I am hopeful. I know that the church can become something different than it is now. It will because it must. The church is a remarkable institution! It has always managed to listen to the music of God and to dance to that new music. The American nation is wrenching its way to a new reality. The signs are all around us. There is reason to be frightened of a postmodern world. So much is up for grabs. No single moral or spiritual truth seems able to gain the upper hand. Moral chaos could ensue. Too much freedom is a dangerous thing.

Here enters the new church of Jesus Christ in a postmodern world. It will not stand at the center of its culture. It will not be able to legislate Christian morality. It will not even remain the source of the central religious story by which Americans have interpreted their reality. People will no longer confuse moral behavior with Christian faith. Instead, moral laws and rules will emerge from a variety of sources—courts, various religions, family, common respect.

The church of Jesus Christ in a postmodern world can become again what it once was—a group of people who live on the margins of society and who live out the faith from that cultural edge. Its voice can again become a prophetic voice calling for change in the world. It can preach that freedom has its limits, and it can insist that those limits begin and end with Jesus Christ.

It *can* become all of these things. And I hope that it will. Too much hangs in the balance. Too many churches want to stumble along. They are content. Church is good enough for them, so it must be good enough for everyone. They would rather fight than switch.

That is all well and good, except for a small, haunting voice I cannot ignore. It is the voice of a child. It is the voice of God's future church.

"Daddy, church is boring."

Is there anything more to it than what we witness in most traditional churches on a Sunday morning?

Ah, but it's just a child, you say. Children always find church to be a bit tedious. And you are right, except for the fact that most everyone seems to find it boring just now. They've all wandered over to the county fair to check out the shamans and monks and goddesses.

Meanwhile, here we sit in the ruins of the cathedral, scratching our heads and pointing fingers at the traditionalists or the progressivists or whoever it is we blame for this sorry state of affairs. Perhaps this time we should listen. We can build as we go. We are midwives in the process of birthing God's new church. We can keep what works and get rid of whatever fails to work.

We have obligations. Behind us stands a great cloud of witnesses who once fashioned new churches out of the ruins of old ones. All around us sit people who desperately need renewed spirituality and a community of faith out of which to make sense of their lives. And, in front of us, a future church awaits. It expects to find us faithful.

Note

[1]Loren Mead, *The Once and Future Church: Reinventing the Congregation for a New Mission Frontier* (New York: The Alban Institute, 1991. 1994 ed.) 5.

Bibliography

Abbot, Abiel. "Traits of Resemblance in the People of the United States of America to Ancient Israel: In a Sermon Delivered at Haverhill, On the Twenty-eighth of November, 1799, The Day of Anniversary Thanksgiving; Haverhill, Massachusetts, 1799." *The American Republic and Ancient Israel.* Ed. Moshe Davis. New York: Arno Press, 1977.

Albanese, Catherine L. *America: Religions and Religion.* 2d ed. Belmont CA: Wadsworth Publishing Co., 1992.

Allen, Diogenes. *Christian Belief in a Postmodern World: The Full Wealth of Conviction.* Louisville KY: John Knox Press, 1989.

Ammerman, Nancy T., ed. *Southern Baptists Observed: Multiple Perspectives on a Changing Denomination.* Knoxville TN: University of Tennessee Press, 1993.

———."Organizational Conflict in the Southern Baptist Convention." *Secularization and Fundamentalism Reconsidered: Religion and the Political Order.* Vol. 3. Eds. Jeffrey K. Hadden and Anson Shupe. New York: Paragon House, 1989.

Andersen, Hans Christian. *His Classic Fairy Tales.* Trans. Michael Foreman. New York: Doubleday & Co., 1974.

Anderson, Leith. *A Church for the 21st Century.* Minneapolis MN: Bethany House Publishers, 1992.

Anderson, Walter Truett. *Reality Isn't What It Used to Be: Theatrical Politics, Ready-to-Wear Religion, Global Myths, Primitive Chic, and Other Wonders of the Postmodern World.* San Franciso: HarperSanFrancisco, 1990.

———, ed. *The Truth about the Truth: De-Confusing and Re-Constructing the Postmodern World.* New York: G. B. Putnam's Sons, 1995.

Antoun, Richard T. and Mary Elaine Hegland. *Religious Resurgence: Contemporary Cases in Islam, Christianity, and Judaism.* Syracuse NY: Syracuse University Press, 1987.

Appleyard, Bryan. *Understanding the Present: Science and the Soul of Modern Man.* New York: Doubleday, 1993.

Barna, George. *The Barna Report: What Americans Believe.* Ventura CA: Regal Books, 1991.

———. *Virtual America.* Ventura CA: Regal Books, 1994.

———. *What Americans Believe: An Annual Survey of Values and Religious Views in the United States.* Ventura CA: Regal Books, 1991.

Barnes, Samuel H. *Politics and Culture.* Ann Arbor MI: Institute for Social Research, 1986.

Barth, Karl. *The Word of God and the Word of Men.* New York: Harper Torchbooks, 1957.

Bediako, Kwame. "Jesus in African Culture: A Ghanian Perspective." *Emerging Voices in Global Christian Theology.* Ed. William A. Dyrness. Grand Rapids: Zondervan, 1994.

Bellah, Robert N. et. al. *Habits of the Heart: Individualism and Commitment in American Life.* San Franciso: Harper & Row, 1985.

Berger, Peter L. *A Far Glory: The Quest for Faith in an Age of Credulity.* New York: Anchor Books, 1992.

Buechner, Frederick. *Wishful Thinking: A Theological ABC.* New York: Harper & Row, 1973.

Carroll, Jackson W. *Religion in America: 1950 to Present.* San Francisco: Harper & Row, 1979.

Carter, Stephen L. *The Culture of Disbelief: How American Law and Politics Trivialize Religious Devotion.* New York: Basic Books, 1993.

Coates, Joseph F. "The Highly Probable Future: 83 Assumptions about the Year 2025." *The Futurist,* January 1995.

Cox, Harvey. *Religion in the Secular City: Toward a Postmodern Theology.* New York: Simon and Schuster, 1984.

Crouch, Andraé. "Soon and Very Soon." *The Baptist Hymnal.* Nashville: Convention Press, 1991.

Bibliography

Dawn, Marva J. *Reaching Out Without Dumbing Down: A Theology of Worship for the Turn-of-the-Century Culture.* Grand Rapids: Eerdmans, 1995.

Dockery, David S., ed. *The Challenge of Postmodernism: An Evangelical Engagement.* Wheaton IL: Victor Books, 1995.

Dyrness, William A., ed. *Emerging Voices in Global Christianity.* Grand Rapids: Zondervan, 1994.

Ferguson, Duncan S., ed. *New Age Spirituality: An Assessment.* Louisville KY: Westminster/John Knox Press, 1993.

Gallup, George, Jr. and Jim Castelli *The People's Religion: American Faith in the 90s.* New York: Macmillan, 1989.

Gerard, Susan Elizabeth and Judith Stacy. " 'We Are Not Doormats': The Influence of Feminism on Contemporary Evangelicals in the United States." *Uncertain Terms: Negotiating Gender in American Culture.* Ed. Faye Ginsburg and Anna Lowenhaupt Tsing. Boston: Beacon Press, 1990.

Ginsburg, Faye, and Anna Lowenhaupt Tsing, eds. *Uncertain Terms: Negotiating Gender in American Culture.* Boston: Beacon Press, 1990.

Gordinier, Jeff. "On a Ka-ching! and a Prayer: In the Wake of 'Gump', the Entertainment Industry Gets Spiritual and the Profits are Heaven-Sent." *Entertainment Weekly,* 7 October 1994.

Grenz, Stanley J. *A Primer on Postmodernism.* Grand Rapids: Eerdmans, 1996.

———. "Star Trek and the Next Generation: Postmodernism and the Future of Evangelical Theology." *The Challenge of Postmodernism: An Evangelical Engagement.* Ed. David S. Dockery. Wheaton IL: Victor Books, 1995.

Hadden, Jeffrey and Anson Shupe. *Secularization and Fundamentalism Reconsidered: Religion and the Political Order.* Vol. 3. New York: Paragon House, 1989.

———. *Televangelism: Power and Politics on God's Frontier.* New York: Henry Holt & Co., 1988.

Hammond, Phillip E., ed. *The Sacred in a Secular Age.* Berkeley CA: University of California Press, 1985.

Hauerwas, Stanley, and William H. Willimon. *Resident Aliens: Life in the Christian Colony.* Nashville: Abingdon Press, 1989.

Herberg, Will. *Protestant, Catholic, Jew.* Garden City NY: Doubleday Anchor, 1960.

Hinson, E. Glenn. *The Integrity of the Church.* Nashville: Broadman Press, 1978.

Horgan, John. *The End of Science: Facing the Limits of Knowledge in the Twilight of the Scientific Age.* Reading MA: Helix Books, 1996.

Howe, Neil, and Bill Strauss. *13th Generation: Abort, Retry, Fail?* New York: Vintage Books, 1993.

Hunter, George. *Church for the Unchurched.* Nashville: Abingdon Press, 1996.

Hunter, James Davison. *Culture Wars: The Struggle to Define America.* New York: Basic Books, 1991.

——. *Evangelicalism: The Coming Generation.* New Brunswick NJ: Transaction Publishers, 1990.

Inglehart, Ronald. *Culture Shift in Advanced Industrial Society.* Princeton NJ: Princeton University Press, 1990.

Johnson, Benton. "Liberal Protestantism: End of the Road." *The Annals of the American Academy of Political and Social Science* 80 (July 1985): 39-52.

Johnson, Ronald W. *How Will They Hear If We Don't Listen? The Vital Role of Listening in Preaching and Personal Evangelism.* Nashville: Broadman and Holman, 1994.

Keck, Leander E. *The Church Confident.* Nashville: Abingdon Press, 1993.

——. "The Premodern Bible in the Postmodern World." *Interpretation* 50 (April 1996) 130-41.

Kelley, Dean M. *Why the Conservative Churches Are Growing.* New York: Harper & Row, 1988.

Bibliography

Kennedy, Eugene. *Tomorrow's Catholics, Yesterday's Church: The Two Cultures of American Catholicism*. San Francisco: Harper & Row, 1988.

Kenneson, Philip D. "There's No Such Thing as Objective Truth, and It's a Good Thing, Too." *Christian Apologetics in the Postmodern World*. Eds. Timothy R. Phillips and Dennis L. Okholm. Downer's Grove IL: InterVarsity Press, 1995.

Leach, Michael. "New Thought Catholicism: An Idea Whose Time Has Come Again." *America* 166 (2 May 1992).

Leonard, Bill J. *God's Last and Only Hope: The Fragmentation of the Southern Baptist Convention*. Grand Rapids: Eerdmans, 1990.

———. *The Nature of the Church*. Nashville: Broadman Press, 1986.

———. "Religion in the South: Profiles for the Future." *Journal of the South Carolina Baptist Historical Society* 20 (November 1994).

Lifton, Robert J. "The Protean Style." *The Truth about the Truth: De-Confusing and Re-Constructing the Postmodern World*. Ed. Walter Truett Anderson. New York: G. B. Putnam's Sons, 1995.

Lyotard, Jean-Francois. *The Postmodern Condition: A Report on Knowledge*. Minneapolis MN: University of Minnesota Press, 1984.

Marsden, George W., ed. *Evangelicalism and Modern America*. Grand Rapids: Eerdmans, 1984.

———. *Fundamentalism and American Culture: The Shaping of Twentieth-Century Evangelicalism: 1870–1925*. New York: Oxford University Press, 1980.

Marty, Martin E. "Transpositions: American Religion in the 1980s." *The Annals of the American Academy of Political and Social Science* 480 (July 1985).

McDowell, Josh. *Evidence that Demands a Verdict: Historical Evidences for the Christian Faith*. San Bernardino CA: Here's Life Publishers, 1979.

McGrath, Alister E. *Christian Theology: An Introduction*. Cambridge MA: Blackwell Publishers, 1994.

McSwain, Larry. "Swinging Pendulums: Reform, Resistance, and Institutional Change." *Southern Baptists Observed: Multiple Perspectives on a Changing Denomination.* Ed. Nancy T. Ammerman. Knoxville TN: University of Tennessee Press, 1993.

Mead, Loren. *The Once and Future Church: Reinventing the Congregation for a New Mission Frontier.* New York: The Alban Institute, 1991. 1994 edition.

Middleton, J. Richard, and Brian J. Walsh. *Truth Is Stranger Than It Used to Be: Biblical Faith in a Postmodern Age.* Downer's Grove IL: InterVarsity Press, 1995.

Miller, Perry. *Errand to the Wilderness.* Cambridge MA: Harvard University Press, 1956.

Moore, R. Laurence. *Selling God: American Religion in the Marketplace of Culture.* New York: Oxford University Press, 1994.

Morgan, David T. *The New Crusades: The New Holy Land: Conflict in the Southern Baptist Convention, 1969–1991.* Tuscaloosa AL: University of Alabama Press, 1996.

Nash, Robert N., Jr. "The Influence of American Myth on Southern Baptist Foreign Missions, 1845–1945." Ph.D. dissertation, Southern Baptist Theological Seminary, 1989.

Niebuhr, H. Richard. *The Social Sources of Denominationalism.* 1929. New York: Henry Holt & Co., 1975.

Phillips, Timothy R., and Dennis L. Okholm, eds. *Christian Apologetics in the Postmodern World.* Downer's Grove IL: InterVarsity Press, 1995.

Pope-Levison, Priscilla, and John R. Levison, *Jesus in Global Contexts.* Louisville KY: John Knox Press, 1992.

Regele, Mike. *Death of the Church.* Grand Rapids: Zondervan, 1995.

Richardson, James T. "Studies of Conversion: Secularization or Reenchantment." *The Sacred in a Secular Age.* Ed. Phillip E. Hammond. Berkeley CA: University of California Press, 1985.

Bibliography

Robbins, Thomas, and Dick Anthony, eds. *In Gods We Trust: New Patterns of Religious Pluralism in America.* 2d ed. New Brunswick NJ: Transaction Publishers, 1990.

Roof, Wade Clark and William McKinney. *American Mainline Religion: Its Changing Shape and Future.* New Brunswick NJ: Rutgers University Press, 1987.

Smith, Huston. "Postmodernism and the World's Religions."*The Truth about the Truth: De-Confusing and Re-Constructing the Postmodern World.* Ed. Walter Truett Anderson. New York: G. B. Putnam's Sons, 1995.

Spangler, David. "The New Age: The Movement Toward the Divine." *New Age Spirituality: An Assessment.* Ed. Duncan S. Ferguson. Louisville KY: Westminster/John Knox Press, 1993.

Stiver, Dan R. "Much Ado about Athens and Jerusalem: The Implications of Postmodernism for Faith." *Review and Expositor* 91 (Winter 1994).

Sweet, Leonard. *Faithquakes.* Nashville: Abingdon Press, 1994.

Tapia, Andres. "Reaching the First Post-Christian Generation." *Christianity Today* 38 (12 September 1994): 18-21.

Veith, Gene Edward. *Postmodern Times: A Christian Guide to Contemporary Thought and Culture.* Wheaton IL: Crossway Books, 1994.

Volf, Miroslav. "Exclusion and Embrace: Theological Reflection in the Wake of Ethnic Cleansing.*" Emerging Voices in Global Christianity.* Ed. William A. Dyrness. Grand Rapids: Zondervan, 1994.

Wacker, Grant. "Uneasy in Zion: Evangelicals in Postmodern Society." *Evangelicalism and Modern America.* Ed. George Marsden. Grand Rapids: Eerdmans, 1984.

Weisel, Elie. *From the Kingdom of Memory: Reminiscences.* New York: Summit Books, 1990.

Wertheimer, Jack. *A People Divided: Judaism in Contemporary America.* New York: Basic Books, 1993.

Wesley, Charles. "O For a Thousand Tongues to Sing." *The Methodist Hymnal.* Nashville: Methodist Publishing House, 1966.

Wuthnow, Robert. *Christianity in the 21st Century: Reflections on the Challenges Ahead*. New York: Oxford University Press, 1993.

———-. *Sharing the Journey: Support Groups and America's New Quest for Community*. New York: The Free Press, 1994.

———-. *The Restructuring of American Religion*. Princeton NJ: Princeton University Press, 1988.

———-. *The Struggle for America's Soul*. Grand Rapids: Eerdmans, 1989.

Young, Pamela Dickey. *Christian Faith in a Post-Christian World*. Minneapolis MN: Fortress Press, 1995.